SERENITY'S PRAYER

Asking for Recovery,

Surviving Our Daily Struggles

Serenity's Prayer

ASKING FOR RECOVERY,
SURVIVING OUR DAILY STRUGGLES

PETER O.

EAST RIVER / SARATOGA

East River/Saratoga Inc.
20 Jay Street
Brooklyn, N.Y. 11201
1-718-797-4000

Copyright © 1997 Peter O'Brien

Library of Congress Catalog Card Number
97-77034

ISBN: 0-9660003-0-7

All rights reserved.

To order by credit card call toll-free 24 hours a day
1-888-317-5552

Printed and bound in the U.S.A.

DEDICATION

To those
Who doubt, but struggle to believe;
Who fear, but struggle to trust;
Who resent, but struggle to love;
Who fail, but still seek;
And,
Who ask only that their prayers
Be not the print of a sparrow
In the snow.

ACKNOWLEDGEMENT

To Jim Jennings, of East/River Saratoga,
who made this book possible.

To Sean Konecky, Arthur Hughes, and Cindy LaBreacht,
who made this book presentable.

To Hal Durham,
who made this book understandable.

To my wife and friends,
whose support made this book come true.

Thank you,

Peter O.

Contents

FOREWORD ix

PREFACE xiii

A Prayer for Renewal xx

The Serenity Prayer 2

INTRODUCTION 5

    CHAPTER 1 Asking 19

    CHAPTER 2 God 27

    CHAPTER 3 Serenity 39

    CHAPTER 4 Courage 57

    CHAPTER 5 Wisdom 75

    CONCLUSION Gratitude 91

Foreword

We are asleep, unaware of our situation, wrote the Russian Philosopher Gurdjieff. He pointed out that if a man was in prison and was to have any chance of escape, he must first realize that he is in prison. So long as he fails to realize this, and so long as he thinks he is free, he has no chance whatsoever.

One of the ways we lull ourselves into delusion is coming to believe that reality is "out there." We become mechanical and reactive; asleep to our inner spiritual nature. To awaken takes some willingness and effort and that effort can take many forms. There is no one way to get to the "god within...the unsuspected inner resource" that the "Big Book", Alcoholics Anonymous describes. We tend to live our lives from the outside in. But, spiritual growth comes from the inside out. We get busy attacking our problems out there, believing that the solutions to our problems are also out there. But as we know, the answers come from within.

Our creator has put within us the spiritual resources to deal effectively with life. We have the answers inside us. The problem is that our inner spiritual resources are crowded out by the external. To awaken spiritually is to recognize that truth and let go of the things that are standing in the way of the emergence of our spirituality.

As Director of the Renewal Center at The Hazelden Foundation, I learned that often the most important thing we could do for our guests was to facilitate an environment; create space and opportunity so the client could rest and reflect. And, ultimately, to allow the answers within themselves to surface. Weary people would come to the Renewal Center who had been out there trying to "make it happen." Often we would remind them to just "let it happen." It is the gentle process of letting go that helps us to connect with the "god within," the "unsuspected inner resource."

Peter O. helps us create the sacred place where that can happen. Since I have known Peter I have been impressed with his connectedness to the spiritual. His clients have grown through very difficult life challenges with the incorporation of prayers and exercises like those in this collection.

These prayers resonate with spiritual energy that connect and center me. Whenever I face a stressful challenge or need to heal from some wound that life has handed me, I find renewal in these spiritual concepts. These are prayers that I can "mean" not simply prayers that I can "say."

Peter has broken new ground in making effective prayer available to everyone. We need nothing more than the willingness to participate. I am grateful for the spiritual growth I have experienced with these simple but profound ideas.

I believe the same can happen for you.

Beginnings

Whenever I visited New York from Center City, Minnesota, land of the many treatment centers, my first visit would be to Peter O.'s office on West 4th Street. I would always come to Peter with the goal of confirming my own experiences as clergyman and treatment professional; and, I wanted to decompress, lay off some of the burn-out that all of us in the field undergo.

Despite Peter's legendary and authentic desire for anonymity, Peter O. is one of the best known individuals in the recovery field. He is considered a counselor's counselor. He is an accomplished weight-lifter acclaimed for his combination of patience and scholarship. He was once a well-known figure on the roughest edges of the Bowery.

One day with Peter I had been updating our progress at the Renewal Center and how we were developing a Twelve-Step "Renewal model." I said to Peter, "Would you put your own thoughts to paper about what ongoing renewal might look like?"

"Sure," said Peter, "give me half an hour." What he produced is, to me, a prayer that rivals the Saint Francis Prayer for depth, accuracy and power. What has become known as "The Renewal Prayer" is thus the first in this volume. It stands as a firm starting point for enriching and expanding the Serenity Prayer.

The Serenity Prayer: Some Historical Notes

It is still not certain who wrote the Serenity Prayer or even when it was written. Even The AA Grapevine, an official, conference-approved publication of Alcoholics Anonymous, has printed some confusing reports.

An Anglican Church publisher asserts that "variations of the serenity prayer have been in common use for centuries." It has been attributed to the German philosopher Friedrich Christoph Oetinger (1702-82).

The modern "author" is Dr. Reinhold Neibuhr, of the Union Theological Seminary, who is said to have written it in 1932 as part of another prayer.

According to The AA Grapevine: "In 1934 the doctor's friend and neighbor, Dr. Howard Robbins asked permission to use that part of the longer prayer in a compilation he was making at the time. It was published in that year in Dr. Robbins' book of prayers. Dr. Neibuhr says, 'Of course, it may have been spooking around for years, even centuries, but I don't think so. I honestly do believe that I wrote it myself.'"

The Grapevine also printed what it identified as Dr. Neibuhr's "own account" as expressed in a letter to a Sister M. Bernhard Joseph of Mount St. Mary College, Newburgh, NY, April 13, 1964:

"...The circumstances back of the prayer are rather simple. I composed it for our summer church in Heath, Mass. A member of the congregation was the late dean of the Cathedral of St. John the Divine, Dr. Howard Chandler Robbins, who was chairman of the worship committee of the Federal Council of Churches. He asked whether he could use the prayer in his monthly report. The prayer was lifted by the Federal Council and was printed for the soldiers in World War II. After that, Alcoholics Anonymous adopted it, so the prayer has wide circulation, but never in book form. I have never used it in any of my books."

The reported dates are confusing because The Grapevine writes that the prayer came to the attention of an early member of AA in 1939. "He read it in an obituary appearing in The New York Times. He liked it so much he brought it in to the little office on Vesey Street for Bill W. to read. When Bill and the staff read the little prayer, they felt that it particularly suited the needs of AA. Cards were printed and passed around. Thus, the simple little prayer became an integral part of the AA movement."

As it appears in The AA Grapevine, it reads:

"God grant me the serenity
To accept things I cannot change,
Courage to change things I can,
And wisdom to know the difference."

The original version attributed to Dr. Neibuhr is as follows:

"God give me the serenity to accept things
    which cannot be changed;
Give me courage to change things
    which must be changed;
And the wisdom to distinguish one from the other.

In any version and regardless of the history, the Serenity Prayer has become one of the best known—and most effectively utilized—prayers in this century. It is an application prayer, a life-skills prayer; it is not about belief, doctrine or dogma. In a profound sense, it may be the prayer of ultimate faith because it recognizes "God" in the context of "inner resource" as the Power greater than ourselves. To this Power we turn to deploy within us the serenity, courage and wisdom necessary to get through the day.

Hal Durham
Boise, Idaho, 1997

Preface
The Peter Letters

Rainer Rilke's letters carry an edge of profound sadness, steeped in a wisdom won through a hard daily existence. In the months when Peter O. was writing these prayers, he began a series of letters in the Rilke mode; but, his carry an edge of hope. There is no doubt that Peter's life experiences are as difficult as Rilke's—or as difficult as many of you reading this—but Peter has managed to claw his way out of the smothering despondency that Rilke conveys.

The two letters that follow are the perfect segue into Serenity's Prayer proper:

LETTER I

Dear Friend,
What is spiritual recovery?

The surrendering into

> "...that unique,
> not repeatable being
> which at every turning of our life
> we are."
> (Rainer Maria Rilke)

How? Through the principle of anonymity.

Some years ago, while working in an alcoholism detox program, I overheard a conversation on the Detox floor. The words still sound in my ears.

Serenity's Prayer xiii

Two men joked after they ate breakfast.
One grew serious. He asked his fellow patient:
"How many times have you been detoxed?"
"This is my third time," he answered.
"This is my twenty-seventh time," the man responded, "and, they still haven't got me."

I watched this man's face as he spoke; it shone with the light of pride, much like a craftsman pleased with his work. Defiance was his craft.

"They" were the treatment staff and visiting A.A. members.

I learned some months later that this man was found frozen to death in an abandoned truck on a Hudson River dock. All the treatment, all the therapy, all the medication, and all the A.A., did not reach through his defiance. This is the spiritual disease of addiction.

Through the years, I learned that defiance, My defiance, is the soul of the spiritual disease of addiction. So much so, that spiritual recovery is really a "power-recovery." That is:

I let go of belief
That defiance is power, and
I accept the truth
That surrender is power.

In defiance
I am powerless;
In surrender,
I am powerful.

Defiance
empowers the problem
but not me.

Surrender
empowers the solution
and me.

Spiritual recovery begins with failure. It is sustained by failure, but in this failure lies the hope of recovery.

> It begins
> When you tire of failure,
> When you tire of trying,
> When you tire of shame,
> When you tire of pain.
>
> The defiance no longer works;
> The "insanity" no longer works;
> It no longer makes you feel sane.
> Who-I-call-me no longer works.
> Entitlement no longer works.
>
> Peace stays only on the horizon,
> Something always beyond and unreachable.

The context varies, but the pain is the same. Alcohol, drugs, sex, gambling, food, rage, depression, anxiety, or all of these, may be the context, but you learn, one by one, they no longer work.

What's left? The inherent paradox of failure: a heavy emptiness. Spiritual recovery is sustained by failure. Failure takes on a life of its own.

> Left to my powers,
> Hate and injury come quick,
> Doubt and despair fill me,
> Darkness and sadness shrink me.
>
> In these moments,
> The lonely orphan of that
> Shadows within me.

But in this failure lies the hope of recovery. Why? I move outside of myself to find recovery. I am willing to move outside of my intelligence and will to find recovery.

Spiritual recovery begins when I surrender to "treatment." But, it goes beyond, way beyond.

> Gradually,
> From the deep layers within,
> My Self emerges.

Slowly,
More and more,
It takes over my consciousness.

Then,
We re-arrange our inner world
Around this center.

This
leads to a new perception,
Eventually a new identity, a new NAME.
I reframe my world.

I am that which I did not think possible.

Spiritual recovery is the emergence of my Self; this leads to a new perception, which leads to a new life.

But, barriers stand in the way. This is where the work begins. Possibly the most effective barrier to spiritual recovery is bitterness: it blinds us to the new Self. Why?

Bitterness is hate cut in stone, and
stone does not love, yet,
love is so essential to recovery.
But, bitterness holds me from loving.

Bitterness holds on to hurt.
It turns hurt into a weapon, and
If not gentled, eventually into suicide.
It stops me from hope, so essential.

Bitterness clouds my shallow belief with doubt,
Much as the blood of the wounded clouds a river.
It pollutes my faith,
So essential to recovery.

Bitterness,
Like the lie of a friend,
Takes the trust out of recovery, and
Trust is so essential.

> Bitterness robs recovery of joy and simplicity,
> Much as death robs
> The whispered secrets of a dead child.
> Joy and simplicity are so essential.

Bitterness is an attitude, a way of perceiving myself and the world with ill-will, deep-seated resentments, envy and jealousy. It grows from defiance, that is, a refusal to accept, admit, or bear a loss or lack, a grief or disappointment.

In the end, it exposes my frailty. It is not the untidy world nor the beast in me that stops the spiritual. No, it is the deep howl of hurt that has turned defiant and now lingers in embattled exile.

Bitterness, not healed, leads to despair. Despair is the plenitude of bitterness.

If bitterness robs spiritual recovery, despair stops it cold. Why?

> Despair is the scared face of hurt, and
> Behind this hurt is grandiosity, and
> Behind this grandiosity is entitlement, and
> Behind this entitlement is a fragile self-esteem, and
> Behind this fragile self-esteem is fear, and
> Behind this fear is a belief—
> I do not matter.
>
> Despair is the discipline of not-mattering.
> It is the empty soul of not-mattering.
> It is paralysis.
> When paralyzed,
> I don't turn to the "other-than-me."
> So, how can I recover?

The purpose of these letters is to help this not happen, but to move beyond my old identity, my old NAME, to let the deep Self within emerge and to connect to the large Self. From this I will matter. This is spiritual recovery.

LETTER II

Dear Friend,

Some years ago I sat in a smoke-filled room. I was angry. Angry that I could not drink, angry I had to listen to others, angry at the smoke; in fact, I was so angry I lit up a cigarette myself.

Different people spoke different thoughts—some repetitive aphorisms, others very sincere.

After the meeting I was offered my first lesson in spirituality: it was a simple handshake. This handshake reached through my defiance: "My name is ___, can I help you?" No profound words, only his hand, his time and his smile. I have seen this happen many times over many years. Eventually I came to understand what was taking place:

Picture yourself on the edge of a precipice.
You look across a deep chasm.
You wish to get to the other side.
There is a thick rope that spans the chasm.
It is stretched taut.

You swing onto the rope.
You begin to cross.
You hold on with your hands;
each hand crosses over the other.

Fresh and strong, and glad there is a way,
You continue to cross.
But,
Midway your arms tire.

Your hands burn.
You look down.
You are terrified.
Fear sets in: you panic.

Again you look down.
You see only depth.
Your feet dangle.
They stretch to touch, but they simply hang.

The rope cuts your hands.
It pulls on the cuts.
You want to give up.
It is not possible to continue.

On the other side you see a stranger.
The stranger waves to get your attention.
The stranger repeatedly yells:
"Let go! Let go!"

You stay frightened.
The stranger yells:
"There is a glass walk just beneath you."
You look down, you don't see anything.

Again:
"It is only a foot or so beneath you."
You still do not see the walk.
You can't take it anymore.

Again:
"If you let go, you will land on the walk.
You will cross safely."

You chance the belief.
You let go.
Your heart leaps. You are not sure.
But, you land on the glass walk.

You step. You try.
It is true.
You walk across safely.
Even the memory of the pain leaves.

The willingness to recover spiritually is to place my recovery on a path I cannot see, to heed strangers' words, to believe what is outside the boundaries of knowing and chance a mistake, possibly a deadly mistake, by "letting go."

And, yes, the pain does leave. But the memory? No. Now, it is my strength.

A Prayer for Renewal

GOD,
God-of-My-Understanding,
I believe Renewal is an opportunity:
It is a chance to revitalize my life.
Only my arrogance, and
My fear of fellowship stand in the way.
I believe Renewal is a beginning; it is not an end.

R

It is an opportunity, a beginning
To Rearrange my inner life.
It is for this I pray,
Help me to set my feelings,
my thoughts and my will
Around a new center, a deeper Self.

It is for this I pray,
Take me from my surface, deepen me.
This brings pain, yes;
This brings fear, yes;
But, it will bring back to life my life.
Or, it will bring to life my life.
It will restore vitality and vigor
to my inner life.

E

The deeper Self within is unique.
It is unprecedented. It is unrepeatable.

Ancient Greeks spoke of this as a "god."
It was an "en-theos," the "god-within."
From this word came our word: Enthusiasm
Renewal is Enthusiasm
We begin a pursuit of the "god-within,"
This is the ancient meaning.
We bring to this pursuit enthusiasms;
The search is keen, active and ardent.
This is the modern meaning.

The book Alcoholics Anonymous stresses:
"With few exceptions our members find
that they have tapped an unsuspected
inner resource which they presently

identify with their own conception of a
Power greater than themselves."

The "unsuspected inner resource"
Is the "god-within."
As fuel stays in the privacy of the deep earth,
There rivers of fuel flow quietly and
Move through their asylum until tapped.
Then they give warmth and power.

So, it is my prayer
That I tap into my inner deep, my inner Self,
That moves in the marrow of me.
This inner Self
Wills to unfold me,
Wills to be me,
Wills to live me:
To be this unique life.
This "will" is God's Will for me.
It is "tapped" through silence and surrender.

Help me to bring Enthusiasm to this pursuit.
I will find Your Will for me
In Your Will is Renewal.

N

I will find Renewal through
The Principle of Anonymity.
Help me to grasp this principle.
The source for the word is Greek:
It means "nameless."
"an" - without
"onoma" - name
A "name" distinguishes one person from another,
one place from another,
one thing from another.
For us, "name" refers to the idea that we have of
ourselves that distinguishes me from others.

It answers:
How I identify "me" to myself,
How I describe "me" to myself,
How I evaluate "me" to myself,
What I associate to "me" as "me".

Serenity's Prayer **xxi**

The Principle of Anonymity refers
To letting go
Of those answers to these questions that block
"the pursuit of god within," and
"tapping unsuspected inner resources."
That stands in the way of Renewal.

GOD,
God-of-My-Understanding,
Help me to surrender my old thinking about my

NAME

Nature:
The basic beliefs I hold of me,
The basic beliefs I learned about me,
The basic beliefs I keep to myself,
They direct me.

Autobiography:
The memories I select,
The memories I favor,
The memories I prefer,
they control me.

Margins:
The limits I restrain me with,
The lines I enclose me with,
The room I confine me to,
They identify me.

Expressions:
The voice I speak with,
The sound you hear,
The stance I take.
They give flesh to my beliefs,
my memories and my traits.
In Renewal, I am willing to surrender my NAME.

E

Help me to Explore my inner world.
There are assets in my NAME,
They nourish me.
I will Explore how to develop them.
There are liabilities in my NAME,
They poison me.
I will Explore how to dig out these
inner, frozen weeds;
hardened and fixed.

If the Principle of Anonymity is the
spirit of Renewal,
then the heart of Renewal is fellowship,
and the limbs of Renewal are silence and surrender
I will explore my NAME.

W

Low self-Worth stalls recovery.
When my Worth lacks vigor,
Then, I am in want of Renewal.
When I explore this,
I find that I am holding onto beliefs,
Basic beliefs about me, my NAME; then
My prayer is clear.
I ask to let go of my attachments
To those beliefs stunting me.
I ask the God-of-My-Understanding:
Wash me of these beliefs—Especially:
"I do not measure up,"
"Everything about me is a failure,"
"I lack what is necessary,"
"Everything about me is lacking."
They live so deep in me,
My prayer is clear:
I ask for the Gift of Anonymity;
Anonymity brings self-Worth.
Anonymity frees me. When free,
Then I will believe that no matter what
was conveyed to me yesterday,
today, power over my Worth is mine,
And the Fellowship of Renewal that nourishes this power.
With others, my power is not boneless.

Also: through Renewal I learn:
Self-Worth builds upon acceptance and action.
If I am held by low self-Worth,
I ask two questions:
What am I not accepting about me?
What actions am I not taking?
Acceptance and action harbor worth.
In them are refuge and shelter, protection and
security for my Worth.

Renewal of self-Worth begins in fellowship,
And grows through acceptance and action
And "tapping the unsuspected inner resource."
Then, I will find the God-of-My-Understanding,
The foundation of my Renewal.

Serenity's Prayer xxiii

A

When enthusiasm leaves my inner world,
I lose my tie to my outer world.
The connection to a world-larger-than-me dies.
I lose Awe
It is then I need Renewal.
Beliefs and memories I select from my life
direct and control me.
I pray for the Gift of Anonymity:
To be freed of these beliefs.
that have become my NAME.
Deep within me is the belief
that the world is a place "I am thrown,"
Dice have more hope than my life.
Deep within me is the belief that "I have been cheated."

Then, the bitterness sets in, much as winter
And in winter, we hide,
And if I am to hide
I need to get small.
It is no wonder I feel trivial.

Only through Anonymity will I be free.
In Renewal I will find Anonymity. And,
it will restore Awe.
Why Awe?
Awe signals that the universe centers not on me;
Awe signals firm conviction that I am not thrown;
Awe signals an opening of my inner world;
in a word,
Awe opens the envelope my ego.

This is my prayer:
Let me connect to a world-larger-than me.
I no longer want to be trapped and
forced to an obedience that denies me.
I no longer want to fear moving outside my border,
beyond my world, my margins.
There is a world behind the world I see,
Let me reach it.

L

When I lack Love,
and all is cold;
when Love dims, and awkward looks take its place,
and I am worn down from loneliness,
I need Renewal
Since Renewal is Love

The greater my need for Love,
The greater my fear of Love.
The fear makes the need.
In Renewal, Love begins with fellowship.
If Anonymity leads Renewal,
much as the head leads the body, and
I f acceptance and action are the limbs,
Then fellowship is the heart of Renewal.

My prayer is that I be open to fellowship,
and not closed to it.
So often the thought of being open is followed
by the thought of loss.
But, what will I lose?
Only an image of myself that no longer works.
A belief that is no longer useful.
A NAME I no longer want to answer.

I ask in prayer that I fear not Love,
nor hold on to shame,
A shame that covers me,
The shame of soul-nakedness.

I ask in prayer that the "god-within" the
"inner resource,"
rises as a tide within and
as a tide, covers the dry world within.

GOD,
God-of-My-Understanding
I ask that my Renewal be a learning:
That I learn Silence to find the "god-within,"
That I learn Acceptance to free the "god-within,"
That I learn fellowship to feed the "god-within."
And all will take place only
When I learn to surrender my sense of Entitlement,
My belief that "I am entitled to be Special,"
Because this keeps me from the truth:
"I am special."

Peter O.

SERENITY'S PRAYER

Asking for Recovery,

Surviving Our Daily Struggles

The Serenity Prayer

GOD,
God-of-My-Understanding,

You are to me as my *Ground*
I ask only to *Open*
As a seed in You and
Grow in the *Deep* of all things.

To do this,
Let me move beyond my ego to Your world, and

Grant me the *serenity* to accept what I cannot change,
Grant me the clarity

To *Surrender* what my *Ego* holds onto, and
To accept what my *Self* is fitted for;

To surrender what was, my *Resentments*, and
To accept my past hurts;

To surrender what will be, my *Expectations*, and
To accept Your expectations;

To surrender what is, my *Narrow-vision*, and
To accept the large-vision of Your world;

To surrender what could have been, my "*If onlys*," and
To accept my past decisions;

To surrender my talents, my fear of my *Talents*, and
To accept my "fit" into Your Will;

To surrender my growing-up, my *Yesterdays*, and
To accept my growing-up as it was.

Grant me the *courage* to change what I can, especially
Grant me the courage to love, this means

Let me shift what I *Center-on*, in order
To listen not just to me, but others;

Let me climb over any *Obstacles*, in order
To listen without defenses;

Let me replace my *Uniqueness*, in order
To listen to the others' uniquenesses;

Let me look beyond *Rejection* from the other, in order
To listen to the fear of rejection in the other;

Let me turn to a new set of *Assumptions*, in order
To listen to the others' assumptions;

Let me trade in a *Gossiping* tongue, in order
To listen to the pain in the other.

In it all, I ask to *Endure* in my struggle to love.
Grant me the *wisdom* to know the difference:

Let me *Waken* to Your world—within and without;

Let me grow in a "learned *Ignorance*":

Let me be willing to *Share* my "learned ignorance";

Let me *Dare* to reach beyond my truth;

Let me learn from the *Ordinary*; and,

Let me learn from *Meditation*.

As a result,
I will know what to accept,
What to change.

Introduction

Prayer asks only for an open heart:
a heart entirely ready to give and receive,
a heart that does not fear to beat.

What Is Prayer?

Prayer is talk made sacred, inner talk.

It is like any other talk, it differs only in the direction: the "Who" addressed.

If I am able to speak to my sponsor, a counselor, I am able to pray. If I am able to speak to my father or mother, my husband or wife, my lover, my children, my friends, I am able to pray.

Prayer is a simple turning: the gift of speech turns towards the Giver-of-Speech.

In prayer I speak my soul. I take the cover off. I lift the lid on my soul. The more open the talk, the more authentic, the more I will be touched, and the more I will touch.

In prayer I give my *Self* through talk, sacred talk, and, in return, I receive my *Self* as gift.

Prayer is rooted in language—the sounds and gestures. So, like language, prayer is a spectrum with many prisms, many variations, and much diversity.

There is formal, public prayer—structured, ritualized, and common to all. Different traditions sanction different public prayers.

There is informal, private prayer—spontaneous and immediate. A wonderful example is the prayer spoken by the English leader Sir Jacob Astley on the morning of the Battle of Edgehill in 1642:

> "Lord, You know how busy I must be this day,
> If I forget You, do not forget me!"

This is simple, human "talk." It could be said to many, but it wasn't: it was directed to the Lord; this made simple inner talk sacred.

It is this spirit that is the spirit of this book. The content of the prayers arise out of the content of my sessions as a counselor for over thirty-five years. I might add, for some of those years, I also shared the contents.

What Do I Say?

Since prayer is rooted in language, and language is rooted in all that is human, so *all that is human* is the "talk" of prayer.

At times the talk of our prayers will be like that of an infant crying for safety; or that of a child, direct and somewhat self-centered; or that of the young, a mixture of joy and fear; or that of lovers, grateful and committed; or that of the aged, gazing at the past and wondering about the future.

Prayer is the "talk" of the life cycle.

At times the talk of our prayers will be that of hunger, a longing for nourishment, a thirst for a better life; or that of rage and resentment as we struggle with love and forgiveness; or that of questions and doubts as we struggle with faith and belief; or that of despair, darkness, and sadness as we struggle with hope, light, and joy; or that of praise and gratitude as we struggle to look up and not down.

So, what do we say?

All the above! I change not a word, only a direction.

For us, our "talk" will be through the words and spirit of the recovery program of Alcoholics Anonymous, especially as stated in the *Eleventh Step*:

> Sought through prayer and meditation to improve my conscious contact with God *as we understood Him*, praying only for knowledge of His will for us and the power to carry that out.

"*Asking for recovery*" is simply asking through prayer,
1. to improve my conscious contact with God-as-I-understand-Him,

6   Serenity's Prayer

2. to ask *Only* for knowledge of His will for me,
3. to ask for the power to carry that out.
   Why?
   This *is* recovery: the carrying out of God's will for me: The "me" I am meant to be!

Why Pray?

A problem is not solved by a problem.

If something is the problem, it cannot also be the solution. I must go outside the problem to find the solution.

The *only* problem to my recovery is "me": *The "I" that I learned to call "me."*

To "solve" this problem, I must go outside of "me" for the solution.

I "go out" through fellowship, meditation, and prayer.

Horizontally, I "go out" through "fellowship": sharing my inner world with others, individually and in a group.

Vertically, I "go out" through "prayer and meditation." In meditation, I go within and down-deep; in prayer, I go without and up-high.

So, why pray?

Prayer is a solution to the problem of recovering from "me." It takes "me" out of "me," out of my arrogance, willfulness, anxiety, resentments, and the poor opinion I have of "me."

"Serenity's Prayer" solves the problem of "me."

How?

When I "ask for recovery" I let go of my dependence on my intelligence, will, and feelings. The "letting go" heals my arrogance.

When I "ask for recovery" I let go of my decisions based on my intelligence, will, and feelings. This "letting go" heals my willfulness.

When I "ask for recovery" I am willing to trust what is outside my intelligence, will, and feelings: I am willing to listen. This "letting go" heals my anxiety.

When I "ask for recovery" I am willing to clean my intelligence, will, and feelings from hate; I am willing to forgive. This "letting go" heals my resentments.

When I "ask for recovery" I am willing to receive what my intelligence, will, and feelings say I am not worthy of! This "letting go" heals the poor opinion I have of "me."

The "old me" keeps closed the doors of recovery; prayer opens these doors. Prayer, like searching fingers on a flower, helps me to touch my recovery. For this I am grateful. In fact, gratitude leads all reasons for "Why pray?" since prayers of gratitude are the keys to the doors of recovery.

What Blocks Prayer?

If talk is simple, why is prayer hard?

Doubt, distractions, and despair make prayer hard.

DOUBT

Prayer speaks to *someone*. It is not a simple repetition of words; it is grounded in a belief, in a direction.

Our beliefs may vary, our metaphors and similes may differ, but, prayer holds that there is a "Power-greater-than-and-other-than-ourselves."

Without this belief, prayer at best is a set of positive affirmations. At worst, it is "me-talk" filled with superstition and magic.

Many of us doubt a "Power-Greater-Than-Ourselves." This blocks prayer since it sees prayer as "childish," and the rewards of prayer not much more than "candy."

We break through this block when we turn this "doubt-talk" into "prayer-talk."

Since "doubt" is so common, many of the prayers found in this book will attempt to turn "doubt" into "prayer." Doubt need not be frightening, since doubt brings trust to faith. One way or another, our prayers will say:

"Lord, I believe, help my unbelief."

DISTRACTIONS

Distractions draw me away from prayer.

This is the "noise," inner and outer, that turns my inner talk away from the direction of the *"sacred."* These are the sticks, roots, and trees that change the flow of my prayer-river.

The "outer noise" is from the world around us; the "inner noise" is from the world within us.

"Inner noise" is the wind and storm of "me-talk"—worry, resentments, and lust. These three draw our "inner talk" away from the direction of prayer.

But, if we take literally that prayer is "inner talk made sacred," then even distractions become prayers. As we will see, this "me-talk" can be turned into "prayer-talk."

However, there is an exception—"dishonesty." It is the great distraction in prayer. I am "dishonest" in prayer when my prayer is not authentic, not real, I am not praying the truth of this moment; rather, I pray with "denial." My praying is "make-believe."

If I am angry, I deny my anger; if I am lustful, I deny my lust; if I am envious, jealous, I deny my envy and jealousy; if I am greedy, I deny my greed; if I am bitter, cynical, and sad, I deny my bitterness, cynicism, and sadness; if I am proud, I deny my pride. I make believe that "all this" is not me. This is dishonest, it cannot be turned into prayer.

Why?

Because this "noise" takes the blood from prayer, and if life loses blood, it dies. Prayer is no different, it also dies.

Really, I just need ask myself:

What lover prizes "dishonesty" in the loved?

What poet praises a "dishonest" poem? Or,

What parent asks for a "dishonest" request?

If this is so, why should the God-of-My-Understanding be offered "dishonesty?"

There is absolutely no inner talk that cannot be made into prayer, except "dishonesty." It is our prayer that no prayer in this books lacks "honesty."

DESPAIR

What would it be like to lay my head on the "Chest" of God?

But, this question is often followed by others: "Does this God really care for me?" "Sure there is some 'Higher Power,' but, does this 'Power' care for me?" "Can I risk that God is on my side?"

With questions like these, discouragement is only a step away, and despair is only a step away from discouragement.

Despair is real. It blocks prayer.

Despair is like a fingerless blindman who is unable to hold on any more. Prayer is no longer a growing tree, but a stump.

In despair all is distant, shriveled, and sour; so is my prayer, if I pray at all.

In despair "life" bites hard—too sharp for kisses, and too

tight for hope. So, why pray at all. Prayer is too steep. I stay absorbed in my wounds, often shattered by the artillery of betrayal; I submit to despair. I don't care about prayer.

Despair stops prayer *only* if we stop talking. Again, we turn "despair-talk" into "prayer-talk." I talk of my despair, I ask it to be "lifted"—to "God" my despair is a veil hiding me, but to me, it is granite entombing me.

This will be the theme of many of our prayers. If despair is my inability to keep up with the pace of God's Will for me, then prayer is the request for that speed.

Nowhere is this seen better than in the Psalm-prayer No. 130 as found in the Judeo-Christian Scriptures. It reads:

> Out of the depths I have cried to You, O Lord;
> Lord, hear my prayer!

Another translation, not literal, but holding to the sense of the words, would be:

> Lord,
> Out of the darkness of my prison,
> The never-ceasing sadness and emptiness,
> I beg You to hear me,
> No, I yell for You to hear me.
> Please. Do not betray me!

Is there a better example of "despair-talk" turned into "prayer-talk?"

If "dishonesty" takes the blood from prayer, "despair" takes the soul.

Doubts, distractions, and despair feed on themselves, while prayer brings me out of myself to myself and others.

Who Is the "Who"?

Prayer speaks to a Higher Power, a Power perceived as Sacred, a Power-Greater-than-and-Other-than-Ourselves. It is towards this Power that prayer is directed. Since this Power is Sacred, it is what makes our inner talk sacred.

This Power is not like any other power: It is truly Outside-the-Ordinary. It is Special, if It were not, It would not be a Higher Power. Because this Power is beyond any looking or hearing, we must go to figurative language—metaphors and similes—to speak of this Power. It is beyond what can be experienced fully.

In the spirit of Alcoholics Anonymous, we come to this Power in our own way. Because of this, we speak of the God-of-Our-Understanding. Obviously, there is only one Power, otherwise it would not be outside the ordinary; but, we reach this Power through different paths. We use different figures of speech, hence the idea: the God-of-Our-Understanding.

This is seen clearly in the Judeo-Christian Scriptures where there are many figures of speech—some masculine, some feminine, some neither—that attempt to explain the Unexplainable.

What is most important is not to confuse the metaphor with the Reality. If we do, we lose the sense of a Higher Power for It is no longer outside the ordinary, no longer special.

Even words like Power, Intelligence, Will, and Feelings, when used to attempt to explain the Higher Power, the Unexplainable, are metaphors: they are like what we know them as, but they also differ vastly.

Still, we come to see this Power as real. This Power is made Real, not by magic and superstition, nor by illusions and hallucinations, nor by premises and syllogisms, but by wonder, awe, and mystery. This Power is made Real by my experience of littleness before the Largeness of this Power, by the experience of my powerlessness in the absence of this Power, and by the experience of my recovery.

This Realty grows as my skill grows—the skill of moving through my life with unscaled eyes. Some call this faith.

This Sacred Power remains puzzling.

I am able to speak of this Sacred Power, Higher Power, with words and images, with scenes and stories, with examples and experiences, but only to the boundary that ends with me. Beyond this margin, there are secrets not able to be learned.

One secret that continues as a puzzle, as an enigma, is "Why does this 'Power' allow evil?" Maybe the answer, if any, is in the enigma itself!

We do not want to forget, this Power functions as an Intelligence that is outside my strata, outside my grasp. Further, this Power is Autonomous, Self-Governing, therefore, functions outside my will—the Will of my Sacred Power is not necessarily my will.

It is this Power that prayer addresses.

In prayer I am aware that this Power is the Energy that moves the Universe, and it is my hope that this Energy will move the universe within me.

The great irony of this Power is: It does not have power over my will to surrender.

This fact brings to mind a scene that took place some years ago in a detox program.

Two patients, after breakfast, were playfully tossing a hard-boiled egg back and forth.

One patient said to the other, "How many times have you been detoxed?"

The other patient responded, "Twice."

Taking his turn, he asked, "How many times have you?"

Patient No. 1 answered, "Twenty-seven times, and *they still have not got me!*"

The following winter, Patient No. 1 was found frozen to death in an abandoned truck on a West Side dock in New York City.

It is this self-destructive defiance that stays as the great irony in the spiritual life: no one, controls, has power over, my will to surrender. We match wills with the Will of God.

Even though the cold ocean and the scorched-bald desert are under the control of this Power, our defiance—the disguise of hurt—is not.

Maybe our defiance is not as destructive as the above example, but "God" may cajole, push, pull, drag, and even "kick," but my defiance need not give in—"God" still has not got me!

Putting It All Together

Prayer builds from six blocks. Although not always present at the same time, they define prayer.

They tell us:

How to pray?

P—PRESENCE:

First, we silence our inner world. A number of methods may be used: breathing exercises, centering on a collective religious symbol, a personal spiritual symbol, or one that is neutral, such as the flame of a candle. Posture often readies us for prayer, hence, the suggestion to kneel.

What is most important: I allow my *Self* to be aware of a Presence.

In this silence, we allow ourselves to be aware of the God-of-My-Understanding, my Higher Power, the Sacred.

In this silence, we will see what we did not see before: a new intensity where in letting go of our scales, we awaken to a new movement in what we call the world.

In this awakening, the immediate response is praise and gratitude for this Presence.

R — RECALL:

Secondly, I recall the purpose of my prayer:

> ". . . to improve my conscious contact
> with the God *as we understand Him* . . ."

Prayer is not for me to get my will, nor to fulfill some magical or superstitious practice, but to touch, connect, and communicate with this Presence.

I pray to be lifted as a guest to a new world, to get a glimpse of what is beyond, even remote, but a world that is not a mistake.

A — ASK:

Thirdly, I ask to know God's purpose for me. I ask for the enthusiasm to carry it out.

This purpose and enthusiasm will take the sterility from each of my life-moments, the slack from my rope, and put life into my life.

Y — YIELD:

Fourthly, I will let go of my defiance, doubt, and despair: I will yield.

Just as stones do not make good wings, nor dirges songs for a joyful dance, nor bigotry for freedom, so neither does defiance, doubt, and despair aid me in speaking and listening to the God-of-My-Understanding.

E — EXPLORE:

Fifthly, I will look at different aspects of my spiritual recovery. I will explore God's Will for me.

In this search I will ask to be lifted: my fear of insight, its intimidation; my fear of self-knowledge with its scratch. Most importantly, I ask not to soften honesty through any form of denial.

R—RESOLVE:

Sixthly, I will resolve to bring the results of this prayer to the people and situations of my daily life. I will do this through visualizations and affirmations that I will take to the moments of each day.

Prayer ends as a sunrise, not a sunset.

About This Book

Recovery is about change.

The Serenity Prayer is about change.

Put them together and you have the purpose of this book: Asking for the power to change.

Change what?

I ask for the power to change my defiance to acceptance, my fear to courage, my ignorance to wisdom. This is spiritual recovery.

How? How reach serenity?

Anonymity!

This is clearly stated in both the short and long form of the Twelfth Tradition of the Twelve Step Programs:

> Anonymity is the spiritual foundation of all our Traditions, ever reminding us to place principles before personalities.
> Or,
> And, finally, we of Alcoholics Anonymous believe that the principle of anonymity has immense spiritual significance. It reminds us that we are to place principles before personalities; that we are to practice a genuine humility. This is to the end that our great blessings may never spoil us; that we shall live in thankful contemplation of Him who presides over us all.

Anonymity has many meanings, but for us it will refer to the process by which we extinguish whatever in our learned identity interferes with serenity, acceptance, courage, and wisdom.

Anonymity untangles our ego from the past, from the memories that inhabit our inner space, so that we live in the moment; and, this is the foundation of serenity.

Anonymity, like the waves that wash away sand castles, levels our ego, brings it into contact with reality, and not the illusions of the past. Serenity is not founded on sand castles.

Anonymity will be the foundation of each prayer in this book, since it is the *only* way we will find serenity.

Throughout this book we will speak of "my *Self*" and the ego. What does this mean?

If our inner world is like a circle, "the *Self*" is both the center of the circle and the circle itself, the whole. The ego is a small circle within the larger circle.

The *Self* is like a center since it is the axis or pivot of my inner world, not my ego. The *Self* is the core of my psyche, the deep interior around which spiritual recovery clusters. It is deep within, always outside the hold of consciousness.

The world of my ego is the world of survival, of safety, of adapting and fitting into the immediate world. It is of the surface, the ordinary, sometimes conscious, sometimes not.

At the same time, the *Self* gives its name to the whole circle. It stands for all of me, all that I carry around, all that is within the circumference that is me.

Spiritual recovery, hence serenity, consists in centering on "my *Self*," refocusing from my ego, my identity, and, accepting all that is me.

I accept all, not just the good, nor the bad, nor the beautiful, nor the ugly, but all— the good and bad, the beautiful and the ugly.

The ego is not done away with, it is simply no longer the center, nor all that I think I am.

It may be helpful, as some Jungian therapists often do, to look at the history of our perception of the Solar System; it is a clear example of what is being said.

Once it was thought that the Earth was the center of it all— the Sun, planets, moons, all revolved around the Earth, the center.

In the sixteenth century, a shift in perception took place. It was found that all revolved around the Sun: the Sun, not the Earth, was the center of our system. So much so, that it gave its name to our system: the Solar System.

Spiritual recovery, hence serenity, is like this shift in perception.

If our inner world is like the Solar System: the Sun is my *Self*; the Earth, my ego (my name); the planets, my roles; and, the moons, the darkness within me.

I shift from perceiving my ego, my identity (Earth) from being the center to focusing on my *Self* (Sun); and I accept the whole as an interrelating system—my roles (planets) and my darkness (moons).

The Earth is not done away with, it is no longer the center.

Just as the Sun gives life, warmth, and energy to its system, so does my *Self* to its system if I tap into this rich resource.

The *Self* is not sterile rock, but a resource to give me life. When I touch this *Self*, I grow strong and sturdy, I grow deep, no longer bent on following my old identity.

Further, it is a basic assumption of this book that when I connect to my *Self* within, I connect to the Will of the God-of-My-Understanding for me. God's Will for me is for my ego, my identity, to express my *Self*, not my ego to express my ego.

So, when I ask for recovery, I am asking for my *Self*. But this request implies acceptance, courage, and wisdom, hence, I pray the Serenity Prayer. It is the means and the end of spiritual recovery.

When I pray the Serenity Prayer, I am improving "my conscious contact with God as I understand," I am asking for "knowledge of His will," that is, my *Self*.

When I pray the prayers in this book, I am asking for "the power" to be my *Self*, His Will for me.

A Beginning Prayer

GOD,
God-of-My-Understanding,

Let me see the plainness of it all:
How simple.

Serenity is a moment,
A moment of surrender,
Not being sealed.
It is like the willingness
To hear a chime,
To see a face,
To listen to a voice,
To be touched by a breeze:
It is not a web,
It is lace.

I pray,
I ask for recovery,
I ask for serenity.

Let not surrender
Be caught in the narrow of my throat,
Cramped there.

Let me see You
As the always moving ocean,
Not unknown and scary,
But as a current to take me to serenity —
To know Your Will for me:
This is serenity.

Let Your voice
Be the sound of crashing waves,
A sound greater than my sound.
I need Your Energy,
Your Force,
To carry out Your Will for me.

Let Your healing
Cut the nerve that holds me to doubt:
When I doubt,
Surrender twists into a battlefield,
And eventual death.

So,
I ask for recovery:
Grant me the serenity
To accept the things I cannot change,
Courage
To change the things I can, and
Wisdom
To know the difference.

CHAPTER 1

Asking

In asking for recovery,
I am asking for an "opportunity,"
An opportunity to renew my life.

Serenity
Is in seeing
Each moment as an opportunity.

For what?

R—To *Re-arrange* my inner life, and

E—To do this with *Enthusiasm*; further,

N—To let go of my "old *NAME*," and, in doing this,

E—To *Explore* and develop my talents,

W—To grow in a sense of *Worth*,

A—To be open to *Awe* and

L—*Love*.

In doing this,
I will find serenity,
But,
It will take
Acceptance,
Courage, and
Wisdom.

Asking

GOD,
God-of-My-Understanding,

I believe
Each day is an opportunity for renewal,
A chance to vitalize my life.

I believe
Each day is an opportunity
To rearrange my inner life
Around a new center - my *Self*,
To cluster
My feelings, thoughts, and will,
Around a new axis.

I pray:
Take me from my surface,
Deepen me.

I believe this deep *Self* is
Unique,
Unprecedented, and
Unrepeatable.
This deep *Self*,
Termed in the book *Alcoholics Anonymous*
As an "unsuspected inner resource,"
Waits to be tapped.

I pray:
Let me tap this *Self*
With enthusiasm.

Ancient Greeks spoke of the "god-within,"
The "en-theos."
From this came the word "enthusiasm."

I pray:
Let *me* seek actively
My *Self*-within.

Just as fuel stays in the privacy of the deep earth,
And there flows as a quiet river,
And stays in this asylum till tapped,
And then gives warmth and power,
So,
Let me tap this fuel within,
It moves in the marrow of me,
It waits to be tapped,
To give warmth and power.

Asking

Help me bring enthusiasm to this pursuit:
To unfold my *Self*,
To be my *Self*,
To live my *Self*.
This is Your Will.

I believe
I will find my *Self*
Through letting go of my "old NAME" —
The Principle of Anonymity.

Help me to grasp this Principle;
It is the "foundation" of my recovery.

A name distinguishes
One person from another,
One place from another,
One thing from another.

For us,
"NAME" refers to the idea
We have of ourselves that
Distinguishes me from others.

It is the answer to:
How I identify "me"?
How I describe "me"?
How I evaluate "me"?

The Principle of Anonymity refers
To letting go
Of those answers to these questions
That block

The seeking of the *Self*-within,
The "inner resource";

The seeking of Your Will for me,
And the power to carry it out; and

The seeking of serenity, courage, and wisdom.

In a word,
That in my "old NAME"
That blocks my living a renewed life.

What does this mean?
My "old NAME"?

It stands for
The basic beliefs I hold of me,
I learned about me,
I keep hidden, but still control me,
What is fundamental about me,
my basic *nature*.

It stands for
The memories I hold onto,

Serenity's Prayer

Asking

I select,
I favor,
I prefer, that control me,
My *autobiography*.

It stands for
The limits I restrain my *Self* with,
The lines I enclose my *Self* within,
The room I confine my *Self* to,
The *margins* I live within.

It stands for
How I *express* my beliefs, memories,
And, limitations.
My voice,
My sound,
My stance.

The foundation of my spiritual recovery
Is in letting go of all the above that block
My "old NAME."
"Anonymity is the spiritual foundation . . ."
And,
The source of the word is Greek;
It means "nameless," "without name."
"Anonymity" is renewal.

I believe
Each day is an opportunity to explore my world,
Especially, my inner world.

My "old NAME" has assets,
They nourish me.
I will explore
How to develop them.

My "old NAME" has liabilities,
They poison me.
I will explore how to weed them out,
I will dig out these inner frozen weeds,
Hardened and fixed.

I believe
Each day is an opportunity
To grow in a sense of worth about my *Self*.

Only a low sense of worth stalls recovery —
It keeps me deprived of a life,
It robs my recovery.

Serenity's Prayer

Asking

I pray:
I ask for the gift of "Anonymity,"
It brings me worth,
It frees me.

I let go of my "old NAME" —
Those beliefs that keep me stunted,
Words like:
"I do not measure up,"
"I lack what is necessary,"
"I'm different, defective!"

I let go of those memories
That prove these beliefs,
Wash me of these experiences.
They live so deep in me.

I let go of my attachments
To my limitations
That result from my beliefs and memories;
How I act out
And express this low sense of worth.

As a result
I accept the fellowship that surrounds me,
The support,
The power that is not boneless,
That tells me of my worth.

I believe
Each day is an opportunity
To grow in awe,
To connect to a world-larger-than-me.

Why awe?

Awe
Signals that the universe
Centers not on me.

Awe
Signals a firm conviction
That I am not thrown into life:
I am more than dice.

Awe
Signals a silence
Within my inner world,
A silence that leads to You.

Awe
Signals
That the envelope of my ego
Is open.

I pray:
For the gift of "Anonymity,"

Serenity's Prayer

Asking

It is the foundation of awe,
It frees me from what blocks awe —
Bitterness.

Like winter,
Bitterness covers and hides;
And,
If I am to be covered and hidden,
I need to get small,
And stay so.
With bitterness, I stay trivial.
The trivial does not bring awe.

There is a world
Beyond the world I see,
Let me reach it.

I pray:
For the gift of "Anonymity,"
It opens my traps,
They force me to an obedience that denies me,
Keeps me from moving beyond my margins,
Keeps me limited,
Keeps me from awe,
From the world that is beyond what I see.

I believe
Each day is an opportunity for love —
To love and be loved.

I pray:
Not to close to fellowship,
Not to shut down sharing, but
Be willing to love and
To be loved.

The thought of loss
So often follows
The thought of sharing.

But, what will I lose?

An image
That no longer works,
A NAME
That I no longer answer to.

What? What will I lose with love?

Asking

Shame!
Yes,
I will lose shame:
The deep sense of being wrong,
Defective,
Stained,
Phony,
Hypocrite.

I pray:
That Your gift of my *Self*,
My "inner resource,"
Rise as a tide within me, and
Cover the dry world within, and,
Cleanse me of the pollutant shame.

Finally,

I believe
Today is an opportunity
To surrender the infant within
For the adult that is Your Will for me.

Serenity's Prayer

CHAPTER 2

God

The *ground* of serenity —
A God that secures

    GOD,

    God-of-My-Understanding,

    You are to me as my *Ground*,

        I ask only to *Open*
        As a seed in You, and

        Grow in the *Deep*
        Of all things.

To do this,

Let me move beyond my ego to Your World;
Let me move beyond my "old NAME" to Your Will;
In a word,
Let me be "Anonymous":

It is the foundation of all.

Serenity's Prayer

God

Only one journey takes me to a new city, a truly new place—the journey inward, and from there, upward.

I journey inward to my center, and from there, I find my circumference: I am a "new NAME." No longer shut-down, nor tone deaf, I answer to a NAME I am just beginning to hear.

As I answer to my "new NAME," I go seeking.

Seeking what?

God.

The "Center that is everywhere, the Circumference that is nowhere." I journey upward, I seek to make "conscious contact" with God.

Too often, my old image of God, like my "old NAME," no longer works. For many of us it was easily burned away since it was straw-stuffed.

Who wants to make "contact" with a God who is like a harness, we would only tire of the rubbing and chafing; or a God who is like lead, who keeps us stuck and back, a God we drag with us; or a God that we stand before as a Mighty Will, who exiles us into darkness.

Clearly, these images separate, they don't connect, they don't heal.

The Serenity Prayer asks that the image of God be real for me, a God-Who-Touches-and-Moves-Me, a God I have come to, not One I lifted off the printed page, stole from others, a theft; but an image that is mine, not *a God that is mine*, for this is illusion, but an image that rings with my voice, is at home in my psyche, a Rope-that-Never-Breaks.

So, I will seek to find the images, the words, the scenes that will "make contact" with the God-Who-Touches-and-Moves-Me, and this I will term the God-of-My-Understanding.

When I make "conscious contact" with the God-of-My-Understanding, I will no longer have a history of trick attempts at surrender, nor difficulty weaving my will into the fabric of acceptance, the gap of hunger will be filled within me—the "God-shaped hole" within.

But, how speak of my "Higher Power?" The Great Spirit? The Power of the Universe? The Ungraspable?

28 Serenity's Prayer

The God-of-My-Understanding
Is like
> A Teacher-Who-Teaches-with-Love,
> A Mother-Who-Teaches-Me-with-Care,
> A Father-Who-Holds-Me-with-Gentleness,
> A Surgeon-Who-Cuts-My-Disease-to-Heal,
> A Lord-Who-Protects-with-Strength,
> A Lover-Who-Wants-My-Love-and-Loves-Me,
> A Judge-Who-Wants-Only-Honesty-from-Me,

Is like
> A Stream-Heard-through-the-Mists,
> A Sheer-Rock-Against-the-Pounding-Ocean,
> A Field-of-New-Grass,

Is like
> A Power-That-Waits-for-Me,
> A Power-That-Frees-Me-from-Superstition,
> A Power-That-Excites-Me-from-Monotony,
> A Power-That-Opens-My-Senses,
> A Power-That-Opens-My-Eyes-to-a-Deep-Vision,
> A Power-That-Defines-My-Contours,

Is like
> One-Who-Ripens-Me-to-My-*Self*,
> One-Who-Unlocks-the-Resentments-Within-Me,
> One-Who-Reconciles-Me-to-My-Darkness,
> One-Who-Is-with-Me-in-the-Evening.

If I am to be touched and moved, the God-of-My-Understanding is One I trust cares for me: without trust our belief goes sour and cold, my throat narrows, and there is no prayer.

Only if I let go of my "old NAME" will I trust. "Anonymity" is the foundation of trust in our Higher Power.

Gratitude signals Anonymity.

Without gratitude, prayer is either a shriek or a squint. A shriek that yells for my way, or a squint that looks narrow at my life, at what I have to be grateful for—my very life.

We begin the Serenity Prayer with gratitude for my very life.

Serenity's Prayer **29**

God

GOD,
God-of-My-Understanding,
You are to me as my *ground*.

One thing I know, I do not make You.
No,
I am not the maker of God.
But I also know:
I do make the images of God!
So, with this in mind,

I will speak of You as my ground
Since, on my journey,
You are like a ground for me.

Just as earth grounds life,
You ground my recovery.
The earth is the source of life;
It sustains and supports life;
It roots and bedrocks life.
Just as earth is to life,
You are to my recovery.

Just as earth is the living source of life,
So You are to my recovery:
My earth, my ground.
Whether from clay or
Life-giving chemicals,
We come from the earth.
It is from earth that we began,
It is our source,
So You are the Source of my recovery.

Just as earth nourishes life,
So You nourish my recovery:
It is on earth that I journey,
Daily, I touch the earth.
I metabolize the earth,
It nurses my life.
The food chain originates from life-giving earth,
So You are the origin of my life-giving recovery.

It is to the earth that I go in the end:
It takes me, the unwilling me,
Defiant, doubtful, and terrified,
And turns me into more life.
I return to my root: life-giving earth.
Without malice, hate, or judgment, in the end,
The earth is present to us all: it receives all equally.
So do You,
Take my death and
Turn it into life—recovery.

God

As earth is the living ground,
The living root,
So You are the living Earth of my recovery:
My ground.

I believe that
Serenity,
Courage, and
Wisdom,
Mark my spiritual recovery —
They are both
Journey and end.

If this is so,
A Source not ego-made is called for.

Why?

My ego can not lead to recovery,
It needs the recovery.
The problem is not the solution.

Why?

My pain does not bring recovery,
It needs the recovery.
My ego,
My root has been uprooted.

I need a
Source of life
Greater than my ego-source.
I need a
Support of life
Greater than my ego-support.
I need a root of life
Greater than my ego-root.

In a word,
I need a new ground,
My ego-ground is desert.

In a word,
I need You,
The God-of-My-Understanding.

I will plant in You
Only when I let go of my arrogance, and
Come to You through "Anonymity."
Arrogance makes prayer weighty and gross,
Anonymity, guileless and light.
And this is the spirit of the Serenity Prayer.

Serenity's Prayer

God

GOD,
God-of-My-Understanding,
You are to me as my *ground*,
I ask only to *open* as a seed in You.

Growth starts as seed and earth touch.
The seed uncovers, and
The earth is direct.
The embryo is plain, and
The earth is forthright.
From the innocence comes growth.
The claim for life opens the seed.

Likewise,
Spiritual recovery starts when I uncover:
When I am direct,
When I am plain,
When I am forthright, when I am innocent.
This is "Anonymity."

And,

In this, I find
Serenity,
Courage, and
Wisdom.

And,

This is life—spiritual life.

I ask:
Open me to the gift of "Anonymity."

A seed needs ground,
Without ground, a seed shrivels.
The ground is not an enemy to the seed,
It is the seed's hope.
The seed trusts the earth.

Likewise,

When I pray the Serenity Prayer,
I ask to be touched.
I ask You to touch me.
Much as the ground touches the seed,
I ask You, as my *ground*, to touch me.

I will not be touched
Unless I open.

I fear opening.

I know a seed opens in darkness,
Its first step to liberty.
The seed opens to the untold, the unknown,
To that which lacks familiar dress.

I know when a seed opens to the ground,
It begets a force called life. And,
It wants life.

I know when a seed opens to the ground,
There is only silence. Yet,
It trusts silence.

I know when a seed reaches out to the ground,
Slowly, ever so slowly,
It reaches light.

So, when I pray the Serenity Prayer,

The seed will be my ego,
The ground, You;
The shell, my "old NAME."

Through "Anonymity,"
The Serenity Prayer turns to life within me.

I let go of what shuts me closed,
Fears that turn needs into identities,
Rigidity that tightens the shell, that keeps Your touch from me.
Old patterns, anachronisms, which no longer work,
That keep me in the past,
That keep the newness locked within
I let go of through "Anonymity."

Through "Anonymity," I no longer
Mistake security for freedom.

Yes, there is risk,
There is the dark and the unknown,
There is silence.
But there is also light and freedom
Since I find my *Self*,
My center,
My circumference.

ANONYMITY PRAYER

I ask to let go of those
Beliefs and memories that
Direct and control me, and
Keep me from" me," and Your Will.

God

Serenity's Prayer

God

GOD,
God-of-My-Understanding,
You are to me as my *ground*,
I ask only that I *open* as a seed in You,
And grow in the *deep* of all things.

I know this well:
What is familiar,
I fear leaving.
Yet,
The Serenity Prayer asks
That I break the shell of the familiar,
My old identity, my "old NAME."

It keeps me stuck to the surface.
I do not enter the deep of things.
I do not sink deep within —
Me, others, the universe.

But,
If I do,
I will be like the man
Who enters a cave and
Finds the ocean.

Imagine —

You enter a cave.
At first, you crawl:
It is a tight tunnel,
Only the smell and weight of wet earth.

You reach forward, you move.
With each move you wonder if you are trapped.

Than, totally unsuspected,
Your arms reach out into a cavern
Cool and silent.

It is new, you hesitate.
You ask:
"Is this an illusion?"
Within the cavern you hear a stream.
You stay by the stream. The terror lifts.
You follow the stream.
It leads to another tunnel:
Much wider, not made of earth, but stone.
The stones are worn and rounded,
Stuck into the ground.
They serve as a grip.

34 Serenity's Prayer

God

I continue to sink deeper into the cavern.
As I sink deeper,
The stream deepens,
It turns into a river.

The fear returns,
You cannot touch the bottom.
You lack control. The river takes you.

But,
As you move, you see light.
The dank smell of leaves.
You hear what sounds like thunder.
You realize:
The river has carried you to the ocean.

The ocean —
The large water pulsating with power —
Waits for your discovery.

This is the deep.
I left the familiar.
I entered a cave.
I found the ocean.

Likewise,

Through "Anonymity,"
I leave the familiar, my "old NAME."

I enter within, deep within,
There I find my center;
When I find my center,
I find my circumference; and,
When I find my center and circumference,
I find You —
Whose "Center is everywhere, and
Circumference nowhere."
I find my God,
The God-of-My-Understanding.

I ask for the power to let go
Of what keeps me stuck to the surface —
My shame, it spellbinds;
Of what makes me comfortable —
The easy, the ritualized.
I ask to see questions as horizons, and
To see that life has lamps.

ANONYMITY PRAYER

I ask to let go of those
Beliefs and memories that
Direct and control me, and
Keep me from "me," and Your Will.

Serenity's Prayer 35

God

GOD,
God-of-My-Understanding,
Let me move beyond my ego to Your world.

A gift not received is not a gift.
I must not hide my face behind my hands
If I am to receive Your gifts of serenity, courage, and wisdom.
I will move beyond my ego, what my ego contains —
My "old NAME."
This walls me in, You out.

At first,
These walls look impossible to scale.
But, as I grow,
I see the walls turn into mirrors —
The walls image my beliefs.
Yet, as I continue to grow,
These mirrors turn to doors.
I am told:
"If You go though, you will find You."
And,
"If You find you, you will find my will for You."

I will go beyond my ego to my inner space.

So,
Let me move beyond my baggage —
Those belongings I travel with.

What baggage?

My "musts"!
They weigh me down.
"I must . . ."
"We must . . ."
"You must . . ."
I move beyond my "old NAME,"
I move beyond my ego,
When I move away from the "musts."
They feed my low self-esteem.

My "shoulds"!
They cut me down.
"I should . . ." "I should not . . ."
I move beyond my "old NAME,"
I move beyond my ego,
When I move away from the "shoulds."
They feed my arrogance.

36 *Serenity's Prayer*

My "dids"!
They drag behind;
I am a draft animal to my ego.
They tie me to shame.
"I did . . ."
"I did not . . ."
I move beyond my "old NAME,"
I move beyond my ego,
When I move away from the "dids."
They feed my prideful guilt.

My "alls"!
They are too demanding.
They bind me to perfection.
"I am perfect all the time."
"I am not perfect all the time."
I move beyond my "old NAME,"
I move beyond my ego,
When I move away from the "alls" and "always."
They feed my fear.

My "abouts"!
Their noise is too distracting.
They wear me down.
"I worry about . . ."
"I am concerned about . . ."
I move beyond my "old NAME,"
I move beyond my ego,
When I move away from the "abouts."
They feed my anxiety.

My "can't be's"!
They are too distrusting.
They close me down.
"This can't be so . . ."
"This is impossible . . ."
I move beyond my "old NAME,"
I move beyond my ego,
When I move away from the "can't be's."
They feed my rigidity.

The more I let go of this baggage
The more I will find serenity, courage, and wisdom.

ANONYMITY PRAYER

I ask to let go of those
Beliefs and memories that
Direct and control me, and
Keep me from "me," and Your Will.

Serenity

GOD,
God-of-My-Understanding,
Grant me the serenity
To accept the things I cannot change

    Grant me the clarity
        To *Surrender* what my *Ego* holds onto, and
            Accept what my *Self* is fitted for;

        To surrender my *Resentments*, what was, and
            Accept my past hurts;

        To surrender my *Expectations*, what will be, and
            Accept Your expectations;

        To surrender my *Narrow-vision*, what is, and
            Accept the large-vision of Your world;

        To surrender my *If-onlys*, what could have been, and
            Accept my past decisions;

        To surrender my *Talents*, my fear of them, and
            Accept my "fit" into Your Will;

        To surrender my *Yesterdays*, especially my growing-up, and
            Accept growing-up just as it was.

Serenity

What is it?

Serenity is clarity.

It is rooted in an old Sanskrit word "sky," or "shine," as in "the sun shines in the sky." Latin adopted the word as "serenus." When a sky or night is clear, bright, and peaceful, it is called "serenus." It is from this, through the French, that our word "serenity" came about.

Through the acceptance of what we cannot change, we clear our inner sky, we have "serenity."

This clarity allows the deep *Self* within to shine through. And, when this takes place, love and gratitude also shine through—this is spiritual recovery.

ENTITLEMENT

If I am not serene, clear within, it is for one of two reasons:

> either I am not accepting my adult entitlement, or
> I am not surrendering my infantile entitlement.

As an adult I am entitled to, have a right to, and a claim on, the respect, recognition, and regard of others, especially those I have a relationship with.

If I do not accept this entitlement by working with it in a non-destructive way, I will not have serenity.

As an infant I am entitled to, have a right to, and a claim on, the full attention of others, especially my parents. I have a right to be the center of their attention, to be special. In a sense I have a right to control others, to have power-over them, otherwise I would not be able to survive.

Some of us hold onto this infantile entitlement even though we are adults. An infant's survival need turns to an adult's power need—power over others, the past and the future, over all that is my life.

If I do not surrender this entitlement, I will not have serenity.

Defiance is the center of infantile entitlement, it resists accepting what I cannot change.

Clarity, serenity, comes when I am willing to surrender this defiance.

However, this is a narrow path. Surrender is not without a struggle.

The struggle is deep and wide—deep as my hurt, wide as my grandiosity.

If my hurt is deep, my hurt justifies my infantile entitlement: because I have been abused, have unfairly suffered, I have a right to hold on to my entitlement.

If my grandiosity is wide, my grandiosity justifies my infantile entitlement: because of who I am, how dare others treat me like this.

Over time, the hurt deepens into hate, and the grandiosity widens into emptiness.

Some of us turn this infantile entitlement into an identity: we defy living as an adult in an adult world.

At the same time, I am entitled to respect, regard, and recognition from others. I am entitled as an adult.

If I do not believe this, don't feel like I deserve this, don't work towards this with others, I also will be kept from serenity. I resist living as an adult in an adult world.

Somewhere I learned "I am not entitled!" Whether within the family, neighborhood, or school, the learning carved deep. Since it was carved by the power of others, I live feeling powerless with others in my life.

Like a raid of crows, these beliefs rob the seeds of my true *Self*. I live a life of murmur and bowing, but beneath I seethe, since my true *Self* lives behind and helpless (or, so I believe).

In The Serenity Prayer I pray to accept my adult entitlement, since this is God's Will for me, and, surrender my infantile entitlement since this is the will of others for me, not God's.

Acceptance gives my voice clarity, a shape, since it is the sound of my true *Self*; defiance clouds my voice, a non-shape, since it is the sound of others.

"Anonymity" is the foundation of acceptance and surrender. Hence, it is the foundation of The Serenity Prayer.

Serenity's Prayer

Serenity

GOD,
God-of-My-Understanding,
Let me surrender what my ego holds onto, and
Accept what my *Self* is fitted for.

This I ask, this I seek:
A gentle inner world.
Recovery starts with abstinence,
It stays through gentleness.

What I hold onto,
This deep sense of infantile defiance,
Continues to shred and torture my inner world.
It leaves no gentleness, and
Without gentleness, there is no serenity.

You know, and I know
All addicts addict to harshness —
Salt to raw hurt.
But, harshness is wearing, I am tired of it,
So, now I ask to surrender this harshness.

To do this,

I will let go of clinging to my old beliefs,
My "old NAME."
When I stick to this NAME, defiantly,
I jam and fix in harshness.

I will let go of my infantile entitlement,
It is the glue of my old identity.
It holds my spiritual disease together.

Recovery is like fixing a window:
The pane of glass may be new,
But, if placed in the old frame,
The view will not change.
It will be the same —
Narrow.

Likewise with recovery —
The new pane of glass is abstinence,
The frame, the margins I lived by,
The limiting perceptions of my "old NAME."
It is through this window frame that I perceive,
My *Self* and others.

The more narrow the frame, the more harsh
With my *Self* and others;
The more wide the frame, the more accepting
Of my *Self* and others.

Serenity

I believe:
Serenity comes when my old frame leaves,
When I surrender my learned limitations, and
Fit into the frame You will for me—my *Self*.

I will no longer hold on to this old frame,
The frame I learned early,
Especially the three "R's" —
The rejection from others,
The ridicule by others, and
The rage of others.
This frame no longer fits;
I am tired of using this old learning
To design my life,
To judge my life, and
To model my life.

I will no longer hold on to the child my childhood taught me,
The child I NAME me, and
Not the adult You will for me.
Fully convinced in my old learning,
I follow—half-blind and dizzy,
Fully convinced it is me.
No matter the misery, I follow the voices:
"You will never measure up."
"You will never be able to . . . ."
"You can't."

There is a grave in each of us, and
Defiance leads to it.
There is a birth in each of us, and
Surrender leads to it.

I ask for this birth,
But, I need Your Hands to be born.
The energy of my old NAME is too powerful,
It is Your energy I need,
With Your energy, I will accept Your Will for me, and
Not my will for me.

I can not change Your Will for me,
I only can defy It.
How do I know if I am defying?
If there is no gentleness in me!

ANONYMITY PRAYER

I ask to let go of those
Beliefs and memories that
Direct and control me, and
Take me away from me and Your Will.

Serenity

GOD
God-of-My-Understanding,
Let me surrender what was, my resentments, and
Accept my past hurts.

Resentments cloud my inner world.
They are to spiritual recovery
What waste is to a river.

Just as a moving river takes soil,
So it also takes waste.
The waste poisons the river.
The river stops breathing.

Likewise, like river waste,
Resentments deaden my recovery,
Deaden the unborn in me:
The "me" I am to be—my *Self*.

Resentments pollute the flow of my recovery.
The "waste" I hold on to:
Past unmet wishes,
Past reaches for dignity, and
Past failed hopes.

When I resent,
I hold on to these past hurts.
The hurts are not metabolized,
Not accepted into my inner world.

The hurt
Is neither swallowed
Nor spit out,
But sticks within as a sign of suspended acceptance,
Of unfinished work.

Still.
Even though resentments deaden,
Keep me in solitude,
I hold on to them.

Why?

They give
The illusion of power,
The illusion of revenge,
The illusion of protection.

Serenity

I still believe:

My resentments are justified.
"Am I not entitled to them?"
"How dare they!"
"I was hurt; it was unfair!"
"I paid a price!"

Yes,
Entitlement empowers resentment
But, it traps spiritual recovery.

Why?
Resentment is a suicide without dying.
Much like certain poisons,
Resentment, at first, tastes good;
But, as it enters the blood
And pumps its way through my life,
It kills.

Why?
Resentments trap me in the past,
Spiritual recovery is in the present.
When I resent, I hold onto the hurt and the experience.
This is what the word means: it takes two Latin words:
"Re"—repeat, and
"Sentire"—to feel, suffer
Or, be affected and influenced by.
The more resentments influence me today,
The more I am trapped in the past.

Why?
Resentments keep me fixed on a recovery plateau.
A boat moves when an anchor is lifted, but
If the anchor is stuck in the muck, the boat does not move.
So with resentments without forgiveness!

There is a wonderful Celtic saying:
There are three sources of new life:
A woman's belly, a hen's egg, and a wrong forgiven.

To reach forgiveness some of us need professional help;
Also, many of us need lots of time.
But, to work on acceptance is to work on forgiveness
And, forgiveness is serenity.

ANONYMITY PRAYER

I ask to let go of those
Beliefs and memories that
Direct and control me, and
Take me away from "me," and Your Will.

Serenity

GOD,
God-of-My-Understanding,
Let me surrender what will be, my expectations, and
Accept Your expectations.

The more I hold on to my "old NAME,"
The more I hold on to my expectations,
Not Yours.
I step into the future
With the footsteps of the past.
Clearly,
To expect new footprints is an illusion,
Since this future is really the past.

So,
Let me begin to enter Your World.
I will step into the future barefooted:
Without cover, without wear.
In doing this,
I am open to Your expectations,
Not mine.

Let me begin to enter Your world.
I will take my *Self*, Your Will for me,
Into the future, and
Not my fears
Of not being heard,
Of not being recognized, and
Of not being loved.
These fears tighten me:
My muscles, my tongue, my gut
But, more than this,
They tighten my soul.

This is projection:
I look to the future with the eyes of the past.
When I project,
The past captures me, and
Suffocates my future.
It chokes "what can be" with "what was."

I die from lack of *Self*.

I become scattered.

I seek relief.

Serenity

Help me not confuse relief
For the answer.

I seek relief from Your Will
By medicating my will.

How?

I medicate with worry.
If worry does not work,
I try anger, or
Food, or
Sex, or
Envy, or
All the above.
This list brings chaos, and
With chaos come hangovers,
A fitting penalty.
Since my *Self* is left in obscurity.

Is it any wonder I ask You for help!
To surrender my expectations, and
Accept Your Will.

What clouds my expectations is an illusion,
A fundamental error —
What I call reality is not reality,
But a vain battle to hold onto the past,
And make this past the future.

This illusion turns to anxiety within,
To a cry within.
It is for this I pray:
I ask to empty the past of its power,
And since this is protected by my fear,
I ask to let go of my fear.

Let me see the future much as a wilderness:
Unknown, uncultivated, and uninhabited.
Let me recall that the wilderness has laws, much law;
It bids me to respect this law.
The law is simple: the wilderness is not mine.
So with the future: it is not mine, it is Yours.
Let me fit my expectations into Yours.

ANONYMITY PRAYER

I ask to let go of those
Beliefs and memories that
Direct and control me, and
Take me away from "me," and Your Will.

Serenity

GOD,
God-of-My-Understanding,
Let me surrender what is, my narrow vision, and
Accept the large vision of Your World.

The more I hold onto my "old NAME,"
The more I hold to a narrow vision,
A narrow thinking.

If my vision is narrow, my serenity is narrow.

So,
I ask for a big soul,
To let go of my timid breathing.

A large vision simply means:
I do not look at the world
Through the eyes of scrawny bitterness, nor
Through the torments of my never-resting ego,
But I am willing to step into
"The Big Story!"

There is a "Story."

It is bigger than my story.
Its beginning, I do not know.
Its end, I do not know.
Its plot, I do not know.
Its characters, I know only a few.

I know only:
I am not the Author.
It is Your Story. And
You are the Author.

When I live "Anonymity,"
I will live in Your Story,
Not mine.
I will be a willing part of the "Big Story."

In doing this,
I will have the bigness
Serenity calls for.
Just as each story has a time and a place,
So do I:
This moment is my time and place
In Your "Story."

Serenity

What is Your Vision for me?

Your gifts tell me Your Will,
They speak of Your Vision for me.

Clearly,
You give me, and all like me,
A three-fold gift:
The gifts
Of intelligence,
Of imagination, and
Of empathy.

No other known life-form
Has this three-fold potential.

So,
I pray:

Let the depth of my intelligence
No longer be for defense, but for discovery;
Let the breath of my imagination
No longer be for failure, but for success;
Let the reach of my empathy
No longer be stunted, but stretched.

Don't let me try to hide Your Bigness
In my smallness.

Too often
I am overwhelmed.
When this happens
Bitterness shrinks my circle.
Your vision leaves me,
Much as the memory of a victory leaves.
What I once saw as peaks, I now see as walls.
What I once saw as buds, I now see as rot.
I ask to let go of bitterness as a protection
In doing so, I will widen my world.

Let my vision widen and widen
So that the world is like an ocean
And the horizon is not feared.

This is serenity.

ANONYMITY PRAYER

I ask to let go of those
Beliefs and memories that
Direct and control me, and
Take me away from "me," and Your Will.

Serenity's Prayer

Serenity

GOD,
God-of-My-Understanding,
Let me surrender what could have been,
My "if onlys," and,
Accept my past decisions.

Neither rivers nor life flows back,
But often my thoughts do!

"If only I didn't . . ."
"If only I didn't mess up."
"If only I listened."
"If only I did more."
"If only I didn't act out."
"If only . . . If only . . . If only . . ."

Reason is placed aside.
In its place
A lonely longing.
"If it had only been different!"

When I think these thoughts,
What happens to me?

The past turns into a formed mold,
A shape that binds me.
I am left no bigger
Than the mold I flow from.
I lack the inner size to be serene.

So,
It is for this I ask:
Let me see the past as steps,
Not as a mold,
But steps in my journey to be "me."

If I see my past as steps,
Not as an illusory mold
I have a choice not to return.

And, since each step is new
I have the choice to go forward.

Yes,
I can go back.
Yes,
My steps curved.
But,
Steps are not a mold, a cast,
They are a direction.
They leave choice.

Serenity's Prayer

Serenity

Often I brood
Regrets weave in and out of my thoughts.
They paralyze me.
I am stopped.

I am a ship that lies frozen in the sea.
As ice stops a ship,
And slowly pins its journey,
And eventually crushes the ship,
So with regrets:
"If onlys" stop my life.
Pin my journey, and
Eventually crush me.

So,
I ask:

Ice fears only warmth —
It melts ice.
It takes away its paralyzing grip.

Help me to bring warmth to my inner world.

How?

Let me recall
The great lesson of the womb —
Gentleness.

Let me bring gentleness to my past:
Let me forgive me.

I surrender my past into Your Hands.

Your Hand is an open Hand,
It is not a fist,
Nor a pointing finger, but,
A gentle Hand —
Gentle with the gentleness of strength.

Through "Anonymity"
I let go of my old ways,
Especially the use of harshness
To validate me.
I did not realize:
Harshness is like the sheets that wrap mummies,
It wraps me in my dead past.
I pray to unwind these sheets. Serenity belongs to the gentle.

ANONYMITY PRAYER

I ask to let go of those
Beliefs and memories that
Direct and control me, and
Keep me from "me," and Your Will.

Serenity's Prayer

Serenity

GOD,
God-of-My-Understanding,
Let me surrender my fear of my talents, and
Accept my fit into Your Will.

All addictions deprive.
All addictions *Self*-defeat.
In this sense,
Addiction is austere:
It lacks compromise.

This is clear with my talents;
Whatever our abilities, skills, our given,
Either they themselves,
Or their fullness,
Addiction will keep unknown.

If I stay addicted,
I stay unachieved —
No exceptions.
I live a hermit to my talents.

Even when the primary addiction leaves,
When the long pain is over,
This trait continues:
I continue to deprive.

Deprive means to rob.
I rob "me" from "me."
I stay a stranger to my *Self*.
What was meant to be a farm,
Turns into a graveyard.
The latent is sapped,
Decay creeps through a rich field.

Many factors cause this decay.

Above all is fear —
Fear of my talents.

Let me not forget,
That my talents are Your Will for me.

This fear says:
If I follow my talents:
"I will stand out!"
"I will be visible!"
"I will be seen!"

Fear of ridicule,
Of rejection,
This is the salt.

Serenity

In a strange way,
I want emptiness.
I do not want to accomplish.

Strange,
Talent twists into a fear;
It is not perceived as a privilege.

Sometimes my recovery is a half-awakening.
It is as waking from sleep in a chair.
My eyes open.
A light shines in the room.
A voice says: "Stand-up."
I stand. I wobble. I look around.
I am in a room.
There is a door.
I move to open the door.
I stop. I feel looked at.
I don't know what is on the other side.
I tighten and tremble.
I don't open the door.

There is no one in the room, yet,
I sense a great eye staring at me.
It is like I am judged.
It is like I am naked and exposed.
I stand and I sit,
I stand and I sit,
I stand and I sit.
I stay in the closed room.
I never open the door.

The door is my talent.
My talent is the Will-of-the-God-of-My-Understanding.
"Anonymity," and only this, will open the door.
So, I pray to let go of my "old NAME."
The NAME that says "I am a fraud!"

When I let go of this fear,
It is like sunlight
Working its way through tangled branches.

So,
I pray for humility—it frees talent.
I pray for gratitude—it develops talent.
I pray for love—it shares talent.
I pray for "Anonymity"—it takes the ego from talent.
Then, I will enter life as a glove: I will fit into God's Will.
This is serenity.

ANONYMITY PRAYER

I ask to let go of those
Beliefs and memories that
Direct and control me, and
Take me from "me," and Your Will for me.

Serenity

GOD,
God-of-My-Understanding,
Let me surrender my yesterdays, my growing-up, and
Accept growing-up as it was.

For me to be clear
To be serene,
I must turn away from lies
Especially the great lies I live with —
"I don't matter!"
"I'm not important!"
"It's not my place!"
"Who me?"

For so many,
My voice sounds like my yesterday:
House,
Neighborhood, and
School,
We grew from.

There is where the great learning took place,
The sacred truths were passed down,
Not only what I believe,
But what I believe about me,
The truths I judge me by.

There comes a time in our recovery
When we look at our yesterdays:
Childhood, youth, teens.

For some of us, our yesterday enhances —
Years that tend to the beauty in our lives,
Memories we go to,
Much as to high grass,
A place to hide and be soft.
If so, let gratitude be our prayer.

For others of us, our yesterday traps —
Years that tend to the horror in our lives:
Abandonment, orphanages, foster homes, divorces,
Death, sickness, alcoholism, drugs, gambling,
Abuse, incest, moving, poverty. The list goes on.
The quiet places, the soft places, were few, if any;
No tall grass, only faces and sounds to run from.
If so, let surrender be our prayer.

Surrender begins for many of us
When we realize our need for treatment,
Our need for help
To clean us from yesterday.

Serenity

But,
These memories trap;
They control me; they lead me.
I know only their power —
Sounds of raised voices, punched holes in the wall,
Dried blood on hand-me-down pajamas,
Memories of incest, sexual abuse, secrets,
Big hands, odors, and no place to run,
Memories of name-calling, ridicule
Called "sissy" and worse . . .

These monuments sink within me.
They may disappear from sight,
But not touch.
They butt into my present.
They abuse the four edges of my world.
They take serenity from me.

I often want to curse You!
I cry:
"Why didn't You hear me?"
Behind each memory there is the plea:
"Please stop!"
"I'm only a child!"
"I'm innocent!"

But, You did not hear me.

Is it any wonder that I ask today:
"Do You really care about me?"

Yet, this trap is more powerful than I.
I can not break out of it.
The pain grows. I am tired.

So, I will try again.
This time, please listen.
My prayer
Is not to forgive yesterday, nor cease my rage;
This is too big, and, I am not ready.
Rather, my prayer is:
"Grant me the willingness to ask for help."
Please,
Do not let yesterday be memorized pain, nor a kept wound,
But a shell to crack and
Meet the beauty deep within me.
A shell is not a coffin.

ANONYMITY PRAYER

I ask to let go of those
Beliefs and memories that
Direct and control me, and
Keep me from "me," and from Your Will.

Serenity's Prayer

Courage

GOD,
Grant me the *courage*
To change the things I can . . .

   Grant me the courage to love

      Let me shift what I *Center* on, in order
         To listen not just to me, but others;

      Let me climb over any *Obstacles* in order
         To listen without defenses;

      Let me replace my need for *Uniqueness*, in order
         To listen to the others' uniqueness;

      Let me look beyond *Rejection* from the other, in order
         To listen to the fear of rejection in the other;

      Let me turn to a new set of *Assumptions*, in order
         To listen to the others' assumptions;

      Let me trade a *Gossiping* tongue, in order
         To listen to the pain in the other.

      In it all, I ask only to *Endure* in
         My struggle to love.

Courage

What is it?

It is many things—

Courage is the willingness not to "pick up" or "act out" even though every cell in my body wants to be touched by a "high."

Courage is the willingness to wait while the "weeds" are taken from my life, the willingness to let my roots take.

Courage is the willingness not to forget "when," the "remember when," and to keep walking, to keep walking in the wind even when I am beyond tears.

Courage is the willingness to continue after "failure," to start a "new day" even at the end of day, to continue when the nights are sleepless.

Courage is the willingness to have belief and trust since belief is a way of knowing without knowing, and trust is a way of trusting without trust.

Courage is the willingness to see the immensity of the sky, the willingness to believe the belief of all peoples, the basic belief of thousands of years that when the seed dies there will be a plant.

Courage is many things, but it always involves the "conquering of fear after accepting the fear," of "not being faced down by despair after accepting the despair," and "not stopped by opposition, hardship, and danger after accepting the opposition, hardship, and danger."

In spiritual recovery, nowhere is this clearer than the willingness to continue listening care-fully to others.

Listening care-fully is not a habit, it is always a choice.

Whether I listen to those who fit my wants or those who fit my fears, the willingness to continue when burnt out, despairing, lonely, or when frightened, opposed, or in danger, demands courage.

The choice to stand present to another takes courage.

This is spiritual recovery; this will be our prayer.

Listening is possible only through "Anonymity." It is the spiritual foundation of listening. In this sense "Anonymity" is courage.

I listen care-fully when I let go of my old identity, my "old NAME," when I let go of my need for a cover, a shield—with listening, a shield is a hearse. I let go of my old belief: "If you see me, you will not respect me. So I will cover me. I will be a role, a game. A not-me." This takes courage to surrender.

I listen care-fully when I let go of my old identity, my "old NAME," so that I am to others a front door to a home, an open front door. I let go of my belief: "My past tells me: Only if I control others, will I be safe." This takes courage to surrender.

I listen care-fully when I let go of my old identity, my "old NAME," and struggle to enter the inner world of the other, not in judgment, nor, necessarily, in agreement, but with empathy. I will let go of the belief: "If I listen, I lose power-over, I love independence." This takes courage to surrender.

The courage to love, care, listen, is simple:

I choose not to run.

I choose not to run from forgiveness. Rather, I listen with forgiveness, not resentment.

I choose not to run from silence. Rather, I listen with silence, not anxiety.

To listen care-fully asks for change, change from my old beliefs, and this takes courage. Yet, this is spiritual recovery.

And, it is this I pray for.

Courage

GOD,
God-of-My-Understanding,
Let me shift what I center-on, in order
To listen not just to me, but others.

There is a world beyond me,
It extends beyond my reach and rule,
It is the world of others,
Those other-than-me.

I pray for the courage
To let go of my need for the other
To be my mirror, rather,
I pray that
They be a pane of glass.

When the center is me,
I am too tangled to care:
The clarity and simplicity of love is lacking.
Illusions enter,
They snare and twist.
For example:
What I call love
Is often really control.
True,
It has the sound and look of love, but
It lacks the center of love
Since it centers on me
Not us.

When the center is me,
My love is like a museum piece.
Age and past value protects it,
Much as a museum piece.
It is of the past,
Since it is of my childhood.
Yes,
This has value,
But, the value of an anachronism.

When the center is me,
Each moment is the same,
It is a repetitive-me.
As a result,
I lose the freshness of each meeting.
Boring and joyless,
Each meeting has no dream in it.

So,
Grant me the courage
Not to center on me,
But us —
Both "me" and the other-than-me.

Serenity's Prayer

Courage

I know the wind can not chase away a shadow,
It cannot drive it away, but
The wind can clear away what brings the shadow.

And,

If my love is shadowed with lust, envy, and greed,
I ask You
To be the Wind
To chase what brings my shadow —
The selfish rattle of mine,
The baying noise that keeps me from hearing others,
The centering on me.

Give me the courage
To let go of my lust.
What is lust?
Glands lead by a hunting ego;
An ego centered on demands, mine;
Demands that lead to momentary force,
But leave with boredom and regrets.

Give me the courage
To let go of my envy.
What is envy?
Talent without gratitude;
A shapeless ego centered on its lack,
But not its gifts.
A lack that keeps me from me,
From my talents, my *Self*.
Envy takes me from my riches.

Give me the courage
To let go of my greed.
What is greed?
A large mouth with a dreaming ego;
Centered on infantile entitlement,
An entitlement that keeps me void and empty.
Greed carries me to destruction.

In the end,
Lust, envy, and greed betray,
Love does not.
When this shadow no longer hides my *Self*,
I will be able to listen.

ANONYMITY PRAYER

I ask to let go of those
Beliefs and memories that
Keep me frightened to listen
To others and Your Will.

Serenity's Prayer

Courage

GOD,
God-of-My-Understanding,
Let me climb over any obstacles, in order
To listen without defenses.

Many obstacles block love.

One that stands out is
Our drive for approval.
It takes honesty from love, and
Puts game in its place.
Winning people becomes my trade.
I forget,
A life driven by approval ends
Like the blackened silence of burned wood.

Another obstacle is
Our drive to control others.
It runs like an unseen current
Through much love, and
Like a current,
Carries us away from love.

But,
One obstacle,
Possibly the only real obstacle,
Is hate.
Some may think this too strong a word,
But, it is no stronger than the word "war,"
And
War is common.
Hate is dislike,
But with depth;
Hate is hostility,
But with intensity;
Hate is aversion,
But with horror.

It is many faced.
Sometimes the intensity is cut off:
Hate is mechanical and unthought,
Much as a butcher chops meat.
This hate is coined genocide —
A word of awesome understatement.
At other times the intensity of hate is loud,
It is with feeling, much as a bomb tears earth.
This hate is coined violence.
It takes place in many places —
In a home, a city, or
"In hidden wooded places."

62 *Serenity's Prayer*

Courage

Still other times,
The intensity of hate is quiet,
But deadly,
Much as the sharp cut of a blade.
This hate is coined suicide.

Hate does not fade like the dead,
No,
More like mange:
It grows and spreads
As the parasites eat away.
Hate puts craze into the world.

Perhaps hate is in us all, perhaps not.
Whatever,

For some of us, it is deep, deep as a grave.
It is my deep secret:
When it is loud, I decry it;
When it is quiet, I deny it.

Hate need not be large and social.

For many of us, it is small and personal —
Someone in our family, at work,
In our Twelve Step Meetings.

Hate is not innate; it is not from birth.
An atmosphere is a must—a nest to incubate in.
Hate is born in hurt —
In a world where I am not acknowledged, nor heard,
Nor approved.
Hate grows in anger. The anger is gagged.
Gagged anger is rage; hate is impotent rage.
Often, unexpressed hate is depression.

Truly,
I ask for the courage to surrender my hate.
I ask for the release from the illusion —
Hate is a substitute for power,
The last asylum for the powerless.
But, hate is weary.

ANONYMITY PRAYER

I ask to let go of those
Beliefs and memories that
Keep me frightened to listen
To others and Your Will.

Courage

GOD,
God-of-My-Understanding,
Let me replace my need for uniqueness,
In order
To listen to the others' uniqueness.

Yes,
I am unique, but not "Unique."
Yes,
The other is unique, but not "Unique."
Only You are Unique, and
It is through Your Power
That I will listen
To my uniqueness and
That of others.

This takes courage;
It is for this courage that I ask.

I am "Unique" when I believe
I am unequaled,
I am unrivaled, matchless, and
I alone exist.
The other does not matter.

I ask for the courage
To let go of this belief.

It is learned well, and the learning stays.
A memory turns into a belief,
The belief turns into a need, *but*
The belief is now no longer a treasure,
It is a pain that is too long.

This is my prayer:
Give me the courage
To break from my alone-world:
The world of my "Uniqueness."
At times,
It is a room so safe and silent
That I do not want to leave.

But, at other times,
It is a moonless and secret room.
This is painful.
In fantasy or memory or both,
I sit in my "Uniqueness."
I sit alone among my triumphs and treasures,
Living in harmony with my ego-created landscape.
But, this has grown into a shrouded night.
I am scared.
I ask for courage.

Courage

This is my prayer.

Give me the courage
To want the care of others,
Their comfort for me.

Give me the courage
To listen
To the others' love for me.

When I let another love me,
I let go of my "Uniqueness."
I am touched
By the uniqueness of the other.

It is so true:
When I hold onto my "Uniqueness,"
I pay a price —
I never know the simple spell of love,
I remain clad in a dream,
Led by the enchantment of sadness,
I remain an alone-child in an alone-world, and
I mutter words that mask fear.
I never see the wild hues of the setting sun,
Since I stay stuck, mud-stuck, in my centeredness.

I ask to replace this "Uniqueness"

With a belief in my uniqueness,
With a belief in the others' uniqueness.
This is bonding,
It is not dependency.

Through the foundation of "Anonymity,"
Let me go beyond the din of my torment,
And joy in the others' joys,
In their victories.

I ask to replace my "Uniqueness"
With a will to listen
To the uniqueness of the other.

This takes courage.

ANONYMITY PRAYER

I ask to let go of those
Beliefs and memories that
Keep me frightened to listen
To others and Your Will.

Serenity's Prayer 65

Courage

GOD,
God-of-My-Understanding,
Let me look beyond rejection from others,
In order
To listen to the fear of rejection in the other.

My fear of rejection separates me from others.

When I fear rejection,

I do not listen,
Nor am I able to care.
I stand defended.
I am circled by the colors of rejection.
I am swayed by my sensitivity.
I am immobilized by this surrounding hem.

I pray to be released from this fear.

When faced with rejection,

I lose the will to love,
I grope and fumble, often rage.
Certainly I argue:
"How dare they!"
"Who do they think they are?"

Too often
I stay silent.
I settle back,
Paralyzed.

The time-locked child,
Deep in my psyche,
Fears.
Consciously or unconsciously,
I listen to "that time when":
I was put down,
Abandoned,
Minimized.
The past swindles the present from me.
And I allow it.

I stay in that place within —
The time-locked child.
I stay in the lonely tower.
I stay on my "great watch" for rejection.

Scared. I need courage.
It is for this I pray.

Courage

With this fear of rejection,
My vision, voice, and faith leave.
In their place is a
Dim-sight and a stolen voice, and
A loss of possible dawns.
There is only secrecy and night—an unread life.

Yes, fear is powerful,
So I ask for Your help.

With fear,
The other looms as one to be avoided
Rather than one to be heard.
If I am to risk a moment that is beyond my will,
Beyond the lived memories that survive from yesterday,
I need a Power greater than my will,
Greater than my lived memories.
I need You.

In that moment,
I will find my *Self*,
Since I will be free
To be my center and circumference.

Rejection is danger.
I am unable to move independently:
I live with eye-alert and soul-alert.
I let the cold of rejection,
The flashes of past hurts,
Stay as pain, injury, and loss.

I evade listening when I cling to this fear.

Let my psyche open as a hand,
Not with sweat and tremble, but
With warmth and love.

I let go of the beliefs of my "old NAME":
"My past is my truth"
"In its grip I will always be!"
So, I stay a watchman—tired and rigid.

"Anonymity" is the foundation of letting go
With it,
The other is not feared, but heard:
I hear the fear in the other.

ANONYMITY PRAYER

I ask to let go of those
Beliefs and memories that
Keep me frightened to listen
To others and Your Will.

Serenity's Prayer

Courage

GOD,
God-of-My-Understanding,
Let me turn to a new set of assumptions,
In order
To listen to the assumptions of the other.

We each have our own laws:
They tell what my joy is, my sorrow,
They tell me what love is,
They tell me what peace is,
They tell me what wonder is.

These are my assumptions.

They move in me;
They speak what my reality is;
They grow out of the ranks of my life.

More often than not,
They hide in me; they stay unseen.

In the beginning
They aid us to survive and adapt,
Some continue to aid us,
While others
Sand-bag us,
They barricade us.
It is these that I pray to let go.

If I listen, listen well,
Listen to my thoughts and words;
If I listen without denial nor defense,
I will hear,
Often as a recluse in my room,
The ring of their lonesome bell.
Their ring demands:

"Nothing in life is fair; I've been cheated!"
"I'm nothing but scrawl on a jail wall!"
"If you are not like me, you are a threat!"
"No one could love me; no one wants to touch me!"
The sound continues; the loathing never stops.

I ask: take this coupling from me,
They lack love; they hurt.

When they fire through me,
I am as bare as desert sand.

I want a new life, new beliefs, new assumptions.
Through "Anonymity"
I will turn to a new set of assumptions.

Courage

Give me the courage to believe
That the other is not me
And,
This is okay.

We share eyes and tongue,
But not the same vision and speech;
We share arms and legs,
But not the same grasp or gait;
We share a brain and a heart,
But not the same truth or love.

My assumptions
Are not necessarily the others'.
Let me see this.
Each is unique.

Give me the courage
To be a student with others,
Not a sculptor;
Take from me the need
To carve others into my wish;
Take from me the belief
That others are my stones.
Rather,
Let me be a student before the other,
Let me see the other
Not as a book to be analyzed,
Not tissue for dissection,
But as one who begins with ignorance —
A true student.
With this
I will learn from the other who the other is!

A student implies future —
Not touched, untapped, even virginal:
Let my sense of the other be such.
To tattoo the other with my designs
Is not my wish.

Fear is love's mutiny: it rises up against love.
It puts a void in love; takes the curiosity from it.
I shrink from what I crave most—love.
The greater my need for love, the greater my fear of love.
With fear, I rust; I stay lame.
I do not listen to the others' assumptions.

ANONYMITY PRAYER
I ask to let go of those
Beliefs and memories that
Keep me frightened to listen
To others and Your Will.

Serenity's Prayer **69**

Courage

GOD,
God-of-My-Understanding,
Let me trade in a gossiping tongue
In order
To listen to the pain in the other.

A safe place is necessary for recovery.
Gossip robs us of a safe place.
It makes unsafe a place meant to be safe.

Gossip starts as a whisper,
Grows to a wind, and
Ends with a force that breaks.

When I gossip,
"A Twelve Step Meeting,"
"A group,"
"A conversation,"
Becomes a window for voyeurs.

Gossip
Is a large tongue
With a small soul,
A snail's voice
With a long range,
A short knife
With a long cut.
In the end it brings pain.

Gossip
Is only a drop,
But a drop of poison kills.

Gossip
Threatens those who battle the surf,
But have trouble standing on the shore.
They need a place
Where they will not be knocked down.

Gossip
Roots in a number of traits:
Arrogance,
Envy, and
Loneliness
Are a few.
But,
In the world of recovery,
The root of gossip is betrayal:
I am unfaithful to a tradition —
The tradition of extending a welcome hand,
And, not a cutting tongue.

Serenity's Prayer

Courage

I pray for the courage
To let go of gossiping;
I pray that I not be foul
While I act as an angel.

Don't let me barter the secrets of others
For my esteem.
Deliver me from this easy and indulgent answer.
The turning of another's pain, or behavior,
Into a satisfaction of my needs
Is really the work of an honorless soul.

So,
I pray.

I ask you to deliver me from gossiping,
From saying:
"Do you know what _____ said at a meeting?"
"Do you know what _____ did while out there?"
"Do you know their marriage isn't working?"
"Do you know that they are having an affair?"
"Do you know . . .?" "Do you know . . .?"
The cant continues.

I ask not to be a part of it.

Gossip is no exception
To the Law of Gravity:
It pulls down the gossiper.
Early
The word "gossip" referred to a sacred bond —
The bond in baptism between sponsor and child.

The connection was with the word "God":
"Godsibb" in Old English, meant godparent.
Eventually,
It applied to the talk of older godparents
As they talked about the young:
"How the young were not like the old!"
(Sounds familiar!)
In doing so
They broke a sacred bond.

Likewise,
When I gossip about others in recovery,
I also break a sacred bond —
The agreement to be there for another,
Another in recovery.

ANONYMITY PRAYER

I ask to let go of those
Beliefs and memories that
Keep me frightened to listen
To others, and Your Will.

Serenity's Prayer

Courage

GOD,
God-of-My-Understanding,
In it all,
I ask to endure.

In my struggle to love,
Let me outlast
The fatigue
That shows when I try to love.
The fatigue is due
To my strain
To change others,
To control others,
To claim others,
Or, simply,
Not care for others.

Let me remember
Only surrender outlasts fatigue.
Surrender is rest.
Surrender is outlasting.

Let me outlast the brooding:
It takes me from people, and
Puts me in my mind.

Let me outlast the ego-talk;
Purge me of these reclusive arguments.
They gather within my head.
They suck me into my grandiosity.

Let me outlast my wooden face;
Let me bring to it a smile —
It brings grace, ease, and style
To my face.

Let me outlast the hate within me.
Let me listen to the other voice.
It is not twisted.
It is the voice of the womb,
The voice before birth, it lingers;
it speaks everywhere and at all times:
"As brothers and sisters, we share blood,
Let us share love!"

Courage is necessary to endure with love;
With courage, I will not bitter-out;
I will not close down my dreams;
I will not tire of love and care and listening.

Courage

I am tired —
My soul moves as a bound body,
Arms and legs tied.

Let me see
That it is my defiance that fatigues me.
It binds me. I lay weary. I do not love.
When weary, I am an empty bed.
My defiance wants this as my moment,
Not Yours,
It takes courage to outlast my defiance.

So, I ask:
Let me endure, let me bear with the fear in others.
The fear that converts into attack, or
Withdraws into rejection, or
Transforms into possessiveness.

Let me endure, let me bear with my struggle.
Let me tolerate my failures into
Anger, lust, envy, and greed.
I ask only to keep trying.
I will find courage in the logic of mortality —
I am flawed,
Cracks and spots flaw my will.
I ask to bear my skids patiently.

Let me endure beyond sensitivity
When I am sensitive, I personalize,
I bring my history into the moment.
It is like a thief since it robs my love.

Let me see that love is not a dungeon,
It is more like earth—a place to grow.
Let me see that love is not an exit,
But a place to enter, not escape through.
Let me see that love is not soundless.
It is a simple sound, but one that must be said:
"Don't panic! I am here for you. I love you."

"Anonymity" is the foundation of love,
Through it
I will not stay as frozen water,
But as warm water,
Willing to flow with the lives of others.

ANONYMITY PRAYER

I ask to let go of those
Beliefs and memories that
Keep me frightened to listen
To others and Your Will.

Serenity's Prayer

CHAPTER 5

Wisdom

GOD,
Grant me the *wisdom*
To know the difference.

   Grant me the wisdom to know the difference:

      Let me *Waken*
         To Your world—within and without

      Let me grow
         In a learned *Ignorance*

      Let me be willing
         To *Share* my "strength, hope, and experience"

      Let me *Dare*
         To reach beyond my "old NAME"

      Let me learn
         From the *Ordinary* and

      Let me learn
         From *Meditation*.

As a result,

   I will know what to accept, and
      What to change.

Serenity's Prayer

Wisdom

What is wisdom?

Silence.

Wisdom is silence.

It is the silence of an eye opening, an old eye seeing for the first time. Wisdom is a judgment, a choice, a decision, reached not with the noise of my "old NAME," but with the quiet eyes of "Anonymity." "Anonymity" is the foundation of wisdom.

Wisdom is silence.

It is the silence of a leaf falling. The leaf knows when its time to fall arrives, it simply obeys. Wisdom is a judgment, a choice, a decision reached through acceptance, and not the noise of defiance. Acceptance knows how to wait for the Painter to finish. Acceptance is the foundation of "Anonymity," hence of wisdom.

Wisdom is silence.

It is the silence of a breast held for feeding—full, waiting, and willing. Wisdom is a judgment, a choice, a decision, reached through fellowship, and not the noise of isolation. Fellowship listens, it lacks the craft of arrogance. Fellowship is the foundation of acceptance, hence of wisdom.

Wisdom is silence. It is the silence of a dawn rising—the letting go of night. Wisdom is a judgment, a choice, a decision, reached through surrender, and not the noise of infantile entitlement. Surrender is the foundation of fellowship, hence of wisdom.

So,

I will know wisdom, I will "know the difference" when my judgments, choices, and decisions, are based on "Anonymity," acceptance, fellowship, and surrender.

And,

I will know I have wisdom—the right choice, judgment, and decision—when I have silence.

In silence I will hear, hear the deep within, my *Self*. In this, I will hear the Will, the Large Will, the Will of the God-of-My-Understanding.

76 *Serenity's Prayer*

In this Will is wisdom. Not the wisdom of God, this is too large for my psyche to hold, but God's wisdom for me, and, basically, this is clear: to be my *Self*.

Wisdom is like water.

At first water takes the shape of the earth; it fits to the surface. However, with time, the water shapes the earth, the surface fits to the water.

Likewise with wisdom: at first, it takes the shape of man, it is man-size: it fits me. But, with time wisdom shapes me, it is God-size, I fit the Will of the Maker who willed me.

Growth in wisdom is not easy: it is learning a new set of skills, a new way of looking at my life. Like any skill, it grows from practice—choices made in freedom, not in a rut; decisions made with thought, not as reactions; judgments made with humility, not arrogance.

Above all, we will find wisdom through prayer.

I pray to be Wakened to a world-larger-than-my-ego, to a Will-beyond-my-illusions, and to trust what-stirs-within-me. Then, I will know the difference.

I pray for Ignorance. Not the ignorance of laziness, nor fear, nor lack of knowledge, but the ignorance that is the edge of knowledge, the ignorance that comes from learning, a learned ignorance. Then I will know the difference.

I pray for the will to Share: sharing releases wisdom. When I am loosed and free, the deep within hears the deep within the other. Then I will know the difference.

I pray to Dare: to keep in my psyche the sense of a young traveler. I will brace a world-beyond-my-ego, a world-beyond-my-learned-limitations. Then I will know the difference.

I pray to learn from the Ordinary: color and sound are ordinary, yet they are the stuff of beauty and harmony. Wisdom is in the ordinary moments of each day. Then I will know the difference.

I pray to learn from Meditation: it goes beyond the rust that covers the metal, it goes beyond the ego that covers my *Self*. Then I will know the difference.

Wisdom

GOD,
God-of-My-Understanding,
Let me waken
To a world-larger-than-my-ego,
To a Will-beyond-my-illusions,
To a *Self*-stirring-within-me.

Sleep betrays.
Not the sleep that eases my body,
Frames my dreams,
But
The sleep that narrows my *Self*.

And
What is that?
Dread.
Dread is like sleep in that
I shut down,
Stay under the covers, and
Dream nightmares.
Sure, I am safe from the world.
Yes, I am in pain,
But, I am safe.

However,
There is a price to this sleep:
I shrink.
This shrinking is a betrayal —
I deliver my *Self* over to this dread,
I sell out,
Stay to the surface,
Stay small and held down.

Certainly,
Wisdom is not found under the covers!

Wisdom is large,
Dread, small.
Wisdom does not fit in the narrow.

So, I pray,
I ask to be wakened
To a world-larger-than-my-dread,
Larger-than-my-NAME.
In this world,
I will find the wisdom to know the difference.

I ask to be wakened
To a will-larger-than-my-illusions

Here, I will find my *Self*, and
When I do,
I will know the difference.

Wisdom

Wake me
To a world-larger-than-my-NAME.

Let me listen to the Greek legend of Narcissus.
How he found
A face he loved well,
A face he stared at,
A face he knelt vigil before,
Until the vigil turned into a hermitage.
No matter how much he reached towards the image,
His arms stayed empty, his love stayed empty.
He thought he had found a god,
But he found only his ache, and
This ache was his death.
He was a candle without a wick.

His illusion:
Since the image in the pond was his,
He stayed in thrall to this illusion;
He was not able to see beyond his own identity,
His "old NAME."

I pray
To move beyond my "pond," my image,
My illusions.

How do I find my illusions?
I listen to my ache, my emptiness,
To what brings death to me.
These tell me what I am not letting go of,
What I "stare" at.

I pray to be wakened
To a *Self*-stirring-within-me.
A *Self*,
Exiled by my addiction,
Waits half-made and half-filled
For the horizon of my recovery.
Through years of sleep, the *Self* wants to waken.
I pray to listen.

No longer moored to the loneliness deep within,
No more anchored in my fragility,
No longer willing to live through brooding storms,
The *Self* looks to a large ocean.

No longer a house to me,
I am now a home for me:

ANONYMITY PRAYER

I ask to let go of those
Beliefs and memories that keep me
From my center, my circumference, and
Your Center, Your Circumference—this is wisdom.

Serenity's Prayer 79

Wisdom

GOD,
God-of-My-Understanding,
Let me grow in a learned ignorance,

Not the ignorance of laziness or fear,
Nor lack of knowledge;
But the ignorance that is the edge of knowing,
That which comes from learning —
"How little I know!"
"How much to know!"

In a word,
A learned ignorance.

Wisdom lacks arrogance.
Wisdom is a choice, judgment, decision.
It is as wide as the evidence,
As deep as the premises, and
As accurate as the perceptions.
Since arrogance keeps me
Narrow, superficial, and blind,
I miss the target.
Wisdom is not found in arrogance, with arrogance —
I do not know what to accept, what to change.

Only the teachable find the difference.
Those who seek applause will not find wisdom,
Since their primary goal is not to learn.
They lack the quiet needed to be wise,
To know the difference.

In arrogance,
There is no vision:
Arrogance is preoccupied,
Taken in by one's dreams, and
The preoccupied do not see.

Wisdom searches, looks, explores:
It is open and receptive.
It is the work of an adult.
Arrogance keeps me in the world of infancy,
An infant will not find wisdom, and
An infantile adult will find only their leftovers.

No, none of this works:
Sooner or later
The magnifying glass wins over arrogance, and
I find only in ignorance, a learned ignorance,
The wisdom "to know the difference."

Wisdom

My prayer is:
Let me not fear ignorance.

It is okay to be ignorant,
If it results
From time, study, and experience.
It is from this that I will come to see
"How little I know!"
"How little I *can* know!"

With this conviction,
I am ready to be granted
"The wisdom to know the difference."

My prayer is:

Let me learn and master
My questions,
My doubts,
Without
A fall into cynicism and despair.

I will stay at the edge,
The edge of unknowing.

In this
I will walk more and more to wisdom.

Arrogance stops the hunger,
The hunger for the unknown.
This hunger is a must for wisdom.

Arrogance stops learning.
It takes away the edge of unknowing.
This is necessary to grow, to be teachable.

At the same time
Wisdom is not found sitting back and gloating.
If it is judgment grown from truth, then
Ignorance seeds.

Arrogance shuts the door to wisdom;
Learned ignorance opens the door, and
"Anonymity" is the way through the door.

ANONYMITY PRAYER

I ask to let go of those
Beliefs and memories that
Keep me from my center, my circumference, and
Your Center, Your Circumference—this is wisdom.

Wisdom

GOD,
God-of-My-Understanding,
I pray for the will to share.

Sharing releases wisdom.
Loosed and free,
The deep within me hears
The deep within the other.

When we share our
"strength, hope, and experience,"
I find
"The wisdom to know the difference."
Sharing is the giving and receiving of wisdom.

Sharing says:
"My strength is your strength,
My hope is yours, my experience is yours."
I ask in return
"Your strength, hope, and experience.
Together we will find right judgment."
This is wisdom.

Sharing says:
"I will walk towards you;
You will walk towards me,
Then we will walk together."
This is wisdom.

Sharing says:
"Maybe my hurt will touch your hurt, and
In doing so, we will not hurt so much."
In fact,
"Maybe we will discover how not to hurt."
This is wisdom.

Yet,
Sharing is not magical water
That will simply wash my pain away.
No,
Sharing is work and risk,
The will to let go of my great need —
Not to change.
The work is in the willing,
The risk is in the surrender.

As leather gloves are stiff at first,
But with use they soften to an easy fit,
A fit that protects.
So with sharing:
At first, I am stiff,
But, with use, it wears easy.
It protects.

Wisdom

Often, shame keeps me from sharing.
As a result,
Shame keeps me from wisdom.

Shame keeps me hidden:
It hoards the hidden loathing of mine.
So, I stay deaf to wisdom —
I can't hear through this hoarding.
I can not untie the *Self* within,
I stay snarled and gluey.
I lose the opportunity for wisdom.
Share shame, find wisdom.

But, for many this is difficult.
We carry a darkness within.
A part we do not understand:
It is strange, distant, and other.
It frightens.
More often than not
It speaks of sex and/or violence.
Maybe it is thought, wish, or act;
For some of us it is all three.
When I uncover this part of me to another
— Appropriately and responsibly —
The veil lifts, the hood is off,
And I will be able to see wisdom,
I will begin to see *Self*-esteem
(Maybe for the first time). And
This is wisdom.

Help me to let go of my shame,
Then I will be able to share,
I will find "the wisdom to know."
Let me share my words, and
Not mouth the words;
Let me speak from the belly,
Not ventriloquize in my sharing —
I will not find wisdom in being another's dummy.
Let my sharing
Not be like old clothes and torn pockets;
Let my sharing not be worn war stories,
But the victories and failures of this day.
In this
I will find the wisdom to know the difference.

ANONYMITY PRAYER

I ask to let go of those
Beliefs and memories that
Keep me from my center, my circumference, and
Your Center, Your Circumference—this is wisdom.

Wisdom

GOD,
God-of-My-Understanding,
Let me learn to dare:

To keep in my psyche
The feel of a young traveler, bold;

To brave a world beyond me,
Beyond my margins, my learned limitations.

Wisdom braves *Self*-fulfillment.

Let me learn to dare:

To leave the mapped paths,
To ride the waves, be lifted above the calm, and
Be with the strength of the pulling tide;

To see other lands not as foreign,
To believe in the unseen, and
To descend to the door within and open,
Walk in, through, and about.

Let me learn to dare:

To believe my life is not ashes,
Nor my earth scarred beyond growth;
To believe I am not dead,
That a heart still pounds within me;
To open to possibilities rather than peer at them and
Stay stalled, silent, and alone.

Let me learn to dare:

To lift my *Self* out of bitterness
And to accept that my life,
As the year, has seasons —
Winter ends, but so does summer,
Fall begins, but so does spring.

Let me learn to dare:

To let go of those monotonous nights,
Nights filled with the silent screams of sadness,
Nights when no key worked, and
The nicotine stained shades were pulled down.
To mix joy into the lugging rhythms of my day, and
To finally shed the tears that filled my eyes years ago.

Let me learn to dare:

We are mystery and paradox, but,
With this, I will find wisdom.

Wisdom

Above all,
I ask Your help to dare:
To move beyond my "old NAME," my old identity,
To move beyond my old images,
The words I used to describe me.

I ask Your help to dare,
To move beyond my old judgments,
The values I marked my *Self* with,
The esteem I held my *Self* in.

I ask your help to dare,
To move beyond my old memories,
The hurts,
The mistakes I carry with me.

I ask Your help to dare
To move beyond my old voices,
The voice with no sound,
Yet,
The voice that separates me from others.

In a word,

Let me dare to be "Anonymous."

In "Anonymity"
The mountain top is sought,
Not the cell block,
Nor the measured sounds of my prison,
But,
The freedom to climb,
The freedom to reach beyond my length,
The freedom to see wider than my width,

And find the Great Scope that welcomes.

Here, I will find wisdom,
"The wisdom to know the difference."

ANONYMITY PRAYER

I ask to let go of those
Beliefs and memories that
Keep me from my center, my circumference, and
Your Center, Your Circumference—this is wisdom.

Serenity's Prayer

Wisdom

GOD,
God-of-My-Understanding,
Let me learn from the ordinary:

Color is ordinary,
It is in every moment,
But, beauty is made of color.
Sound is ordinary,
It is in every moment,
But, harmony is made of sound.
Creativity turns the ordinary
To the extraordinary.

Wisdom is
Seeing the ordinary in each moment,
The colors and sound.
Surrender turns the ordinary
To the extraordinary— wisdom.

Wisdom starts where I am:
This time,
This place,
The ordinary.

Wisdom is a way of seeing:
Not the distant,
But what is in my hands;
Not the fantasy,
But the person before me;
Not the abstract,
But the concrete —
What-is-happening-to-me,
What-I-am-experiencing.

Wisdom sees with the belief —
Nothing is ill-timed,
Nothing is accident.
It is always my time. And
When my time conflicts with the Large Time,
I am empty and sad.
The conflict bruises my crude defenses.
Simply,
I forgot that my will
Is not as big as the Large Will.
This is not wisdom.

Each of us has a time and a place —
Our moment.
This moment
Is a gift, a challenge, and a mystery,
It is not a fear.
That is, if I see with wise eyes.
Wise eyes see the ordinary moment
As the Will of the Extraordinary:
Sometimes straight, sometimes crooked;
Only my mutter complains.

Serenity's Prayer

Wisdom

In a time of storm
Even a crooked tree protects;
In a time of thirst,
Even a drink from a wizened hand satisfies.

Likewise,
Wise eyes find wisdom
Even in times of danger and
Times of need.

When I look with wise eyes at the ordinary,
The moment is not seen through my insecurity.
Insecurity is ill-equipped for wisdom;
It keeps me unprepared;
Each moment is spent keeping afloat.
Wisdom does not prosper.

When I look with wise eyes at the ordinary,
The moment is seen as steps towards my *Self*.
When the moment is seen as a step,
It loses friction, there is no rub and burn,
Since I am willing, not resistant.
The moment is a way to arrive,
To arrive to my *Self*.
Wisdom brings me to me.

When I look with wise eyes at the ordinary,
The moment is a living force to be engaged,
Not a memory to be reenacted.
If I see the moment as the Will of my God,
If I do not let insecurity block the moment,
If I see the moment as a step towards my *Self*,
Then, I will engage the moment.
I will not be on stilts in the moment —
Feared of losing control and eventually falling.

Wisdom is the willingness to wait, wait out the storm,
To wait beyond the doubts of broken beliefs,
The God-deserted times,
To see the moment as opportunity,
Full of growth, and
Not muted by past hurts.

Then, I will have
"The wisdom to know the difference."

ANONYMITY PRAYER

I ask to let go of those
Beliefs and memories that
Keep me from my center, my circumference, and
Your Center, Your Circumference—this is wisdom.

Serenity's Prayer

Wisdom

GOD,
God-of-My-Understanding,
Let me learn from meditation.

It goes beyond the rust
That covers my world —
Wisdom is the metal.

Wisdom starts with whispers, and
Meditation hears the whispers.

In meditation,
I go deep within.

At first,
I meet reflections of the world around me —
Mirrors within mirrors within mirrors.
The world of time and place:
Financial worries, responsibilities,
Resentments, sexual fantasies,
And so on —
The nails and spikes
Holding me to the surface.

I go deeper:
I meet reflections of the world within me —
Mirrors within mirrors within mirrors.
The world of past times and places:
Fears, memories, hurts,
And so on —
The cuts forming my NAME.

I go deeper.
Meditation stills these images.
I go beyond the threshold —
The mirrors turn to windows.
I am able to grasp the deeper levels, and
There
I experience my *Self*, I infer my *Self*,
Even if I can not touch my *Self*, hold my *Self*.

It is there, in this deep,
That I hear the underground whispers,
The whispers deep within my inner earth.
It is here where my truth begins.
From here,
I bring forth an ore, and
Through "Anonymity"
The ore transmutes more and more and more
Into my *Self*.

Serenity's Prayer

Wisdom

To be my *Self* is not easy.

Rust starts
When metal is exposed to damp air.
So with the psyche:

When life starts, defenses start.
At first, they serve survival.
With use, they are learned.
They weave into an identity.
This identity is my NAME.

What rust is to metal,
My NAME is to wisdom.

Meditation takes me beyond the rust;
"Anonymity" takes me beyond my NAME.
Through both,
I find wisdom.

Gradually,
As I live a meditative life,
A shift within takes place:
The hooks of resentment break off,
The beatings of shame and guilt disappear,
I find I am able more and more
To release my *Self*.

I go deeper, I discover:
To find victory,
I must surrender.
Wisdom is:
The victory of my *Self*
Through the surrender of my "old NAME."

When I surrender,
I let go of being an ego-made-orphan,
I touch the deep desires that want my recovery.
I tap this resource.
I go deeper than my learning.

Meditation takes me to this resource,
This will to be my *Self*.

ANONYMITY PRAYER

I ask to let go of those
Beliefs and memories that
Keep me from my center, my circumference, and
Your Center, Your Circumference—this is wisdom.

Serenity's Prayer

CONCLUSION

"Gratitude..."

GRATITUDE

Gratitude turns each day into a *Gift*.

Gratitude is the *Root* of spiritual recovery.

Gratitude *Acknowledges*: "I am important."

Gratitude is based on being *Thankful*.

Gratitude *Integrates* my inner world.

Gratitude *Transforms* my identity, my "old NAME."

Gratitude *Unburdens* me.

Gratitude gives me *Dignity*.

Gratitude is *Essential* for spiritual recovery.

Finally: "I am grateful for my failures!"

Gratitude

GOD,
God-of-My-Understanding,

Gratitude is
A position I take towards my life.
It is a way of facing
What happens to me, and
What I happen to be.

It is that state of my inner world
In which
I am thankful to You, my God
I am thankful to my *Self*, and
I am thankful to other Selves.

Thankful for what?
For Your Plan
Which is greater than my plan;
For my *Self*
Which is greater than my "old NAME"
For other Selves
Whose belief is greater than my belief.

Thankful for what?
For my recovery . . .
Why?

Gratitude makes sense of surrender,
It lifts the burden of my defiance.
Gratitude does not betray,
It delivers.
Gratitude takes the wind from my defiance,
It fills me with Your Breath, Your Spirit.
Gratitude takes the rotten-ness from my life,
It fills the hollow in my soul with new life.
Gratitude brings quiet:
When hostility and conflict
Struggle within me,
When my inner war, like all war,
Ends with new war,
Gratitude keeps me from feeling devoured,
It makes life manageable.
Gratitude keeps me connected to my path,
It keeps humility moving.
Gratitude turns scars into living flesh,
It takes our wounds and
Makes the healed healed,
It heals the healing.

Gratitude
Enlivens my life.

Gratitude

At times, gratitude hurts.
It brings harm and pain to my illusions.
It asks me
To let go of the "soundness" of my old beliefs.
It takes the ego-pity from my life.
In doing this,
It offers me serenity, courage, and wisdom.

At times,
Gratitude hurts,
It is hard.
But,
Hard is not impossible.

Gratitude is not my old learned way.
It deviates from my usual responses,
From what I expect of me,
Of others, and,
Of Your Will.
Gratitude is not the voice of my "old NAME."

Gratitude lacks arrogance and disdain.
It takes the arrogance from spiritual recovery.
It says:
"I am not above recovery!"
As a result, recovery happens.

When I am grateful,
I do not look
At my life, nor
Others, nor
Your Plan
With contempt and scorn.

Gratitude needs memory.
It is for this I pray:
Do not let me forget that I am alive,
When with good reason I should be dead.

Gratitude is not bought,
Nor does a bargain make it:
I simply recall the day my recovery began.

Gratitude needs forgiveness.
Especially when I forgive my shame,
Since,
Without shame,
I have the bigness to be grateful.

ANONYMITY PRAYER

I ask to let go of those
Beliefs and memories that block
My openness to gratitude,
To recall and forgiveness.

Serenity's Prayer

Gratitude

GOD,
God-of-My-Understanding

Gratitude turns each day into a gift.

When I am grateful,

I see each day,
Not as a curse, but as opportunity;
I see each day
As rich and fertile for my *Self*, not my illusions;
I see each day
Not as a waste, barren and desert,
Not as a reject, a "good-for-nothing" day,
But as a
Gift.

Gift?

Each day
Is a space in time
For me to be me.

At times,
Each day is more doubt
Than gift; I ask,
"But I don't know me!"
"It is all too much!"
"Everything is a struggle!"

But,

If I live gratitude,
Slowly, ever so slowly,
A quiet grows within me,
My within is easy,
Free and clear from inner storms.
For this to happen,
I need to see my *Self* as part of a plan.
Each day is a moment in this plan.

What happens?

The day moves, it is filled.
All is gift:
Love, but also quarrels,
Joy, but also sadness,
Success, but also failure.
Even our struggles
With lust and greed,
With envy and jealousy,
Since they give such clarity
To my need for You.

Gratitude

When I ask too much of the day,
I lose the sense of gift.
The day is a burden.

When I forget I am clay,
I lose my sense of being human,
The day is a burden.
Gratitude allows me to be human.

Gift implies:

I am not in charge,
Since, if I were,
It would not be a gift.
If I am in control,
It is my will,
Therefore,
Not a gift.

Yet,
Gift does not mean I sit still, and
Expect life to hand me toys.
No.
Gratitude does not trivialize life.
It simply asks that I work with it.

Gift means
Each moment is a meeting:
If I meet another,
I bring love and care;
If I meet You,
I bring surrender; and
If I meet my *Self*,
I bring dignity.

Gratitude knows no seasons.
Winter is as much a gift as summer;
Fall is as much a gift as spring.

Spring is birth, summer is age,
Fall is aging, winter is death.
Each a gift:
Birth, age, aging, and death.
The shallow see chance;
The grateful see destiny.
In fact,
Destiny is the belief: all is gift.

ANONYMITY PRAYER

I ask to let go of those
Beliefs and memories that block
My openness to gratitude,
To recall and forgiveness.

Gratitude

GOD,
God-of-My-Understanding

Gratitude roots spiritual recovery.

Gratitude is not a cliché,
A quick answer to another's plea.
Gratitude is not a whip
To keep people passive.

No.

Like a root,
It is the source of life,
It gathers nourishment for my recovery.

Like a root,
It embeds in my earth.
And,
What is my earth?
My needs and weaknesses,
My failures,
My power-less-ness,
This is my clay, my dirt!

Like a root,
Gratitude fixes in my fraility.
When I root in my frailty with gratitude,
My recovery is solid and strong,
It is not to be dislodged.

This is my power,
Since it makes room for Your Power.
Fragility gets me out of my way.
Lets Your Way happen.
It keeps me from being top-heavy
By keeping me aware of my bottom.

It is through my power-less-ness,
That gratitude, my root,
Takes in Your Power.
With Your Power,
My recovery takes on consistency and growth,

Spiritual recovery
Arises from this alliance.

Gratitude

Gratitude roots my recovery.
Why?

Gratitude roots me in the adult world —
The world of recovery.
It takes infantile defiance from my demands,
And, illusions from my perceptions.
It does not leave me in my inner ghetto.

Gratitude roots me in gentleness —
The soul of recovery.
It does not root in hostility,
Nor bitterness, nor rancor:
These leave teeth tears on my recovery.

Gratitude roots me in life —
The goal of recovery.
It takes the inner smell from my life.
Just as in combat there is a smell,
Of weapons and death,
So deep within many of us
There is also a smell of weapons and death:
We battle with beliefs like,
"I'm a waste!"
"I'm only a pawn!"
"I'm only a card in a gambler's hand!"
"I don't matter!"

All these have the smell of combat.
With them we grow into death,
Into cynicism.
Our recovery stays frozen
Our souls deaf and dead.
Gratitude takes the hidden arrogance
From this combat.
Hence, it gives us life.

So,

There is this request:
Help me root in gratitude.

I know what I don't want,
That is addiction.
It is my analgesic: it numbs and deadens.
I know what I want,
That is gratitude.
It is my freedom: it animates and enlivens.

ANONYMITY PRAYER

I ask to let go of those
Beliefs and memories that
Block me from gratitude and
From recall and forgiveness.

Serenity's Prayer

Gratitude

GOD,
God-of-My-Understanding,

Gratitude acknowledges:
"I am important."

When I say:
"Thank You."
I imply:
"I am important."

Otherwise:
Why give me the gift?

With gratitude, I admit as true that
I have worth and significance,
That my life has consequence.

With gratitude,
With this sense of importance,
I acknowledge that
I am chosen for a task.

Since I am unique,
Unrepeatable in my totality,
My task must also be unique.

My "task"
May still be a mystery,
May still be in doubt,
May take years to find,
But, if I am important,
It implies:
"I have an important reason to be here."

Why should this not be true?
If every cell in my body is appointed to a task;
If every night-dream of mine has a purpose;
If every unit of blood that moves within me has a purpose;
How can I say:
"I do not have a purpose!"
Gratitude acknowledges this purpose.

Further,
Every year I see the wind lift fallen leaves;
Every year I see the day shorten, the night lengthen;
Every year I see buds flower;
This never fails: it repeats over and over.
There must be law; and, with law, purpose.
Why should this not apply to me?
Gratitude acknowledges this purpose.

Gratitude

Too often,
I push You away;
I do not acknowledge the gift.

I say (with words or actions or both):
"How can I be important since I was not important?"
"How can I mean anything since I meant nothing?"
I live with this daily.

I carry a sense that all is unfair,
I have been cheated,
And, it was not my fault.

Daily I take my childhood with me.
With me goes one, or all, of the "three D's" —
Death of a parent,
Divorce of parents,
Dysfunction within my parents:
Drinking, drugging, and abuse,
All seep into my thinking and feeling and acting, and,
Much like dye,
Color my identity, my "NAME."
They paint well:
"How can I be important if they did not see me as important?"
"How can I mean anything if I meant nothing to them?"

It is with this in my soul that
I turn to You with this prayer.

Help me reach beyond the hurts of the past,
Beyond all that I did not ask for!
And reach deep within to the dream within
That no one stills but me;
And reach to light the fire within
That no one puts out but me;
And reach to plant the seed deep within
That no one crushes but me.

With this I acknowledge Your dream for me,
The me You meant for me to be.
The "me" I reach through gratitude.
Please,
Do not let the hurt of the past grind the dream out of me!

ANONYMITY PRAYER

I ask to let go of those
Beliefs and memories that
Keep me blocked from gratitude
And from recall and forgiveness.

Serenity's Prayer

Gratitude

GOD,
God-of-My-Understanding,

When I am grateful, I am thankful. And
When I am thankful, I am truthful. And
When I am truthful, I give credit.
I tell the truth.

The truth is:
I am where I am because others cared!

I left the inertia, the gravity,
The pull of addiction,
Because others cared.
I am thankful.

I left the rut, the rut that dried my soul,
The rut that deepened slowly to a grave,
Because others cared.
I am thankful.

I left the illusions, the snares, the tangles,
The decoys that seemed so real,
So "truthful,"
Because others cared.
I am thankful.

I now believe:
The degree
To which I am thankful,
Is the degree
To which I live life.

In this sense,

Gratitude
Awakes the hero in every man,
The heroine in every woman.

Gratitude
Awakes the seeker, the searcher,
The one who is about the task
Of being them*Selves*.
The one who digs the deep land within,
Who removes the inner earth,
Who loosens the inner earth,
Who uncovers the inner earth
To discover
His/Her *Self*.

For this,
I am thankful.

Gratitude

Others cared for me,
Others care for me,
Others will care for me.
But,
I pushed the care away,
I push the care away,
I will push the care away,
Unless,
I let go of my illusions.

The illusions
That feed my defiance
Of my *Self*,
Others, and
You.

This is so sad since
Illusions are really
Dull,
Boring, and
Repetitive.
They take the brilliance,
The shine from life.

Why?

Illusions are self-limiting.
They cannot let anything beyond them!
They close; they narrow.
But, when thankful, I open my world.
My face tells all
When I am thankful, my mouth curves up, I smile.
When I am defiant, my mouth curves down, I gloom.

Help me to rid my fear of others:

So often I ask You for help.
In return, there is silence.
Let me see another possibility:
You speak to me through the love of others for me.

Is this possible?
Yes!
For this, I am thankful.

ANONYMITY PRAYER

I ask to let go of those
Beliefs and memories that
Keep me blocked from gratitude
And from recall and forgiveness.

Gratitude

GOD,
God-of-My-Understanding,

Gratitude integrates my inner world:
It integrates my inner world
Within my inner world;
It integrates my inner world
With my outer world.

Why?

Integration takes place through acceptance.
When I integrate, I take in,
I unite with,
I make a whole.

How?

When I accept, I receive willingly,
I agree to,
I believe in.
This belief becomes me.

So,
How does gratitude integrate?

When I am thankful, I am accepting —
I accept all the forces within me,
I end the inner segregation.
I am my circumference.

When I am thankful, I am accepting —
I accept all the forces outside of me,
Even if not in my agreement.
But, as I do, I end segregation.
I unite, I make a whole.

Will this take place fully? No.
But,
The more I integrate through acceptance,
The more I heal. I whole. I blend. I tune.
Both the word "heal" and the word "whole"
Derive from a word which meant "complete."

So,
The more I am grateful, the more I am accepting.
The more I am accepting, the more I integrate.
The more I integrate, the more I am complete.
The more I am complete, the more I am whole.
The more I am whole, the more I heal.

All this builds on gratitude.

Gratitude

Help me own *all* of my life,
To integrate all within my life.

Give me the gift of gratitude,

Let me accept failure as well as success
Let me accept weakness as well as strength
Let me accept evil as well as good.

Let me accept my body as well as my mind
Let me accept my enemies as well as my friends
Let me accept my defeats as well as my victories.

Let me accept my lust as well as my love
Let me accept my greed as well as my generosity
Let me accept my envy as well
As my joy for the success of others.

Let me accept my rage as well as my peace
Let me accept my depression as well as my quiet
Let me accept my addiction as well as my recovery.

Let me accept "how I hurt others"
As well as "how others hurt me."
Let me accept the lost jobs and careers
As well as the kept jobs and careers.

Let me accept my regrets as well as my good memories
Let me accept my shame as well as my *Self*-forgiveness
Let me accept my death as well as my life —
However short or long.

When I accept reality just as it is,
I am saying "Thank You."

As I do,
I integrate within—just as it is;
I integrate without—just as it is.

In this, I will find my *Self*.

ANONYMITY PRAYER

I ask to let go of those
Beliefs and memories that
Keep me blocked from gratitude
And from recall and forgiveness.

Gratitude

GOD,
God-of-My-Understanding,

Gratitude transforms my ego.

When I say "Thank You,"
Rather than "Damn You,"
A change takes place within my soul.

I turn from a belief in my "old NAME,"
To a belief in my "deep *Self*."
I am transformed.

I turn from being separate from all,
To being part of all.
I am transformed.

Gratitude is not passive:
It is not an excuse to sit.
Gratitude is a starting line,
It is not a finish line.

When I say "Thank You,"
I say:
Maybe I don't understand this,
Maybe I don't want this in my life,
But, I will not end my life here,
No, I will begin my life, and
I will do this by saying "Thank You."

Begin what?

I will let go of my defiance,
My illusions,
My shadows,
My "old NAME," and,
Let my "deep *Self*" emerge.

As a result:

Gratitude perceives experience
Not as an attack,
But as opportunity.

Gratitude transforms my perception
Of people,
Of places, and
Of things.

Gratitude

When I look within,
It is like looking into a well.

I am like a drop of water
That falls within an unlit well.

Like a drop of water,
I go deeper and deeper,
I sink into the unlit well.

Like a drop of water,
If I hold onto my defiance,
I fall unpitied.
I touch the bottom.
I turn to dust.

In a word,
I say:
"Damn You."

But,

When I say:
"Thank You,"
I am like a drop of water
That falls not into dust,
But, a spring,
A pool, an inner resource.

Like a drop of water,
I enter an underground flow of water,
It connects me to all.

A drop transforms into a stream,
A stream, to a river; a river, to an ocean.
The source is discovered.

This is why I pray for gratitude:
I ask to reach the deep voice within me;
The voice that mirrors Your Voice.
It is through gratitude that I find Your Voice,
In this I will find my *Self*.
And my ego will be transformed.

ANONYMITY PRAYER

I ask to let go of those
Beliefs and memories that
Keep me blocked from gratitude,
Recall and forgiveness.

Serenity's Prayer

Gratitude

GOD,
God-of-My-Understanding,

Gratitude unburdens me.
It takes the staleness from my life:
The musty, closed rooms of my illusions leave,
My life enriches.

When I say:
"Thank You,"
I shake off my arrogance
My feet touch the same earth as others.

When I say:
"Thank You,"
I relieve my ego of *Self*-hate,
My shame is no longer my cargo.
The wounds of shame will heal;
They will no longer curse.

When I say:
"Thank You,"
I lose my anxiety,
I lose my wish to control,
My wish to have power over all.
I lose the sense of impending doom.

When I say:
"Thank You,"
I rid my ego of resentments,
Resentments that have grown into a duty, leave,
They no longer weigh so heavy, nor
Saddle my dreams, nor
Harden my face.

When I say:
"Thank You,"
I clear my ego of depression.
It no longer thickens within me, nor
Tires and jades me, nor
Takes the life from me.
It clears.

When I say:
"Thank You,"
I throw off my rage.
Gratitude gentles me, teaches me to smile,
It takes away my mood, scorn.

Gratitude

Gratitude unburdens my ego.

When I am grateful,
I believe I am "cared for."
Otherwise,
Why say:
"Thank You."
The care for me is shared,
I am unburdened.

When I am grateful,
I believe I "make sense."
Otherwise,
Why say:
"Thank You."
The load of my life is lightened.

Clearly,
Gratitude gives me a depth of freedom.

But,
I question all this!

I ask:
"C'mon, how can the SOURCE of all really care for me?"
"How can this universe that is beyond
Both imagination and mathematics make sense?"

But, it is true! Why?

Because a leaf makes sense!
Try to live on a planet without leaves.
There will be death; life will not be.
If leaves are necessary, then,
A leaf is necessary.
If this is the case, a leaf then makes sense.

If a leaf makes sense, Why not I?

But, I am unlike a leaf in this: I have choice,
I can say:
"Damn You! Life is a flame that burns!" or,
"Thank You! Life is a flame that warms!"
If I choose the latter, life is not a burden.

ANONYMITY PRAYER

I ask to let go of those
Beliefs and memories that
Keep me blocked from gratitude and
Recall and forgiveness.

Serenity's Prayer

Gratitude

GOD,
God-of-My-Understanding,

When I say:
"Thank You!"
Not:
"Damn You!"
I give my *Self* dignity.

What is dignity?

I have dignity:

When I wear my *Self* well,
Not more, not less, and
This is enough;

When I stand my true height,
Not an inch more, not an inch less, and
This is enough;

When I walk not fearing to be seen,
Not concealed, not displayed, and
This is enough;

When I hear my voice,
Not shrinking, not roaring, and
This is enough.

How does gratitude give dignity?

Grandiosity undermines dignity:
It strips dignity, it wears it down.
Gratitude undermines grandiosity.
Hence, it gives me dignity.

Further,

Grandiosity is the name for
The carrying-on of the infant within me:
The distant past still speaks.
My infancy is an unquiet grave!

Gratitude keeps me in the present,
It undercuts the great lie —
I am the center.
In this, it restores dignity,
Since dignity speaks the truth in the present,
Not the truth from the past.

Gratitude

Illusions take dignity from me.

What are the great lies?
"I am the center of it all!"
"I am all-controlling!"
"I am immortal!"

We may not speak these directly,
But they work through and behind —
"How dare you!"
"Don't you know who I am?"
"You can't speak to me like that!"

These lies hawk and peddle
The hunger in my ego,
The beggar in my ego,
The fear in my ego.

Illusions do not give me dignity.

Why?

Illusions wear the clothes of infancy,
They no longer fit.
How can I walk with dignity if my pants are split?
My dress too short?
I will not look dignified in diapers!

But,

Gratitude is not based on the past,
It is not based on a lie,
But, the truth of this moment
Since it is this moment I am grateful for.
I have dignity
When I wear the moment, not the past.

When I am grateful,
I have strength, and
With strength,
Dignity.
No.
My life will not be broken-backed, nor
Erased, nor
A scratch.

Now I have dignity
Since I am grateful for simply being my *Self*.

ANONYMITY PRAYER

I ask to let go of those
Beliefs and memories that
Keep me blocked from gratitude
And recall and forgiveness.

Gratitude

GOD,
God-of-My-Understanding,

Gratitude is essential for recovery.

My goal?
Recovery. Spiritual recovery.

What is it?

The finding of my *Self*, and
The finding of You, and
The finding of others.

How does this happen?

Through "Anonymity" —
The surrender of my "old NAME."

Surrender is essential.
Gratitude is the sign of surrender.
In this sense, it is essential for recovery.
It is basic. It is necessary.

Through surrender
I reach my innermost center.
It is indispensable for spiritual recovery.
Gratitude witnesses this arrival.
In this sense it is essential to recovery.

When I say,
"Thank You,"
The inner waters clear, since my defenses clear.
They lose their necessity.
I am able to see
The undanced me,
The rhythm called me.
Gratitude allows me to *See* my recovery.
In this sense, it is essential to recovery.

When I say,
"Thank You,"
The war is taken out of me,
The so many inner hurdles of fear,
They leave
When I say: "Thank You";
They return
When I say: "Damn You."
In this sense, it is essential to recovery.

Gratitude

Gratitude is essential.

Why?

Gratitude takes me out of my traps.
The snares my illusions set,
They bring confusion.
Gratitude brings clarity.

Gratitude lifts me from defiance,
It topples my arrogance.
They bring disdain and scorn;
Gratitude, warmth and care.

Gratitude evidences humility:
If humility is a sentence,
Then the words are gratitude.

Gratitude helps me to begin anew:
It takes failure from the journey.
All is in the service of gratitude:
Failures, mistakes, wrong turns,
All are the stuff of gratitude
If my arrogance does not nail me to perfection.

Gratitude keeps me in the present:
I let go of my rags,
That which keeps me deprived,
Keeps me empty.

Above all,
Gratitude is the only sure counter to suicide:
It keeps me in life, this life,
It keeps cynicism from dogging me.
If each moment is a view, a horizon,
Gratitude keeps it from being a "hell."

Gratitude is essential.
What oxygen, breath is to the life of my body,
Gratitude is to my spiritual recovery.
It is that necessary.

ANONYMITY PRAYER

I ask to let go of those
Blocks that keep me from gratitude
And recall and forgiveness.

Serenity's Prayer 111

Gratitude

GOD,
God-of-My-Understanding,

Failure is the great secret of recovery.

It takes the swagger from spiritual recovery.
It clearly shows my need for others, and
You.

Failure is
"I do that which I do not want to do."

When I want to be spiritual
But my inner world fills with
Greed,
Lust,
Rage, and,
Depression.

When I set as a goal
To meditate,
But don't.

When I see the force of gratitude,
But think with bitterness.

When I think of my life as
Bankrupt,
Deficient,
Scanty,
As one who is not spiritual.

I ask not to forget:
Failure is the stuff of spiritual recovery.

Why?

Failure takes the arrogance from my recovery,
The strut out of it.

Let me see that
My defects are my greatest asset:
They point to the fact that I cannot do it alone.

The great fault in the spiritual life
Is discouragement.
I turn aside my plans, my projects.
Stamina goes. Confidence leaves.
I lose zeal and enthusiasm for recovery.
I say:
"This spiritual stuff can't be for me!"

Gratitude

Don't let me forget:
Death gives life.
This is the way of the universe,
It is also the way of the spiritual.

Failure without arrogance gives life;
When I own my failure,
I own my neediness;
As a result,
My defiance dies,
My illusions die,
My shadow dies,
My bitterness dies,
My alienation dies,
My sabotaging dies,
My egocentricity dies
And,
In this death,
I find my spiritual recovery.

Let me see:
Spiritual recovery is the craft of placing
One arm around my potential, and
One arm around my failures, and
Bring both to You.

What are we saying?

If I try and fail, and
If I try again and fail, and
If I try again and fail,
If I try again and fail,
Let me see
That the willingness to keep trying
Is real spiritual recovery.

Spiritual recovery says:
God, I am not a saint, and I have no desire to be,
But let me try to follow Your Will, and
Please give me the power to do so.

My failures teach me "Anonymity":
I must get out of the way; and
Let You happen.
I need You to keep my dream alive.

ANONYMITY PRAYER
I ask to let go of those
Beliefs and memories that
Turn failure into failure,
Not into a new beginning.

Serenity's Prayer